TEACHER'S PET PUBLICATIONS

LITPLAN TEACHER PACK
for
Rumble Fish
based on the book by
S. E. Hinton

Written by
Barbara M. Linde, MA Ed.

© 1996 Teacher's Pet Publications
All Rights Reserved

This **LitPlan** for *Rumble Fish*
has been brought to you by Teacher's Pet Publications, Inc.

Copyright Teacher's Pet Publications 1996
11504 Hammock Point
Berlin MD 21811

Only the student materials in this unit plan (such as worksheets,
study questions, and tests) may be reproduced multiple times
for use in the purchaser's classroom.

For any additional copyright questions,
contact Teacher's Pet Publications.

www.tpet.com

TABLE OF CONTENTS - *Rumble Fish*

Introduction	5
Unit Objectives	7
Unit Outline	8
Reading Assignment Sheet	9
Study Questions	13
Study/Quiz Questions (Multiple Choice)	21
Prereading Vocabulary Worksheets	37
Lesson One (Introductory Lesson)	49
Nonfiction Assignment Sheet	54
Oral Reading Evaluation Form	56
Writing Assignment 1	60
Writing Evaluation Form	61
Writing Assignment 2	65
Extra Writing Assignments/Discussion ?s	69
Writing Assignment 3	76
Vocabulary Review Activities	78
Unit Review Activities	79
Unit Tests	87
Unit Resource Materials	123
Vocabulary Resource Materials	139

A FEW NOTES ABOUT THE AUTHOR

Courtesy of Compton's Learning Company

Hinton, S. E. (Susan Eloise Hinton) (born 1950), U. S. Author, born in Tulsa, Oklahoma, in 1950. As a young writer, Hinton decided to write under her initials in order to deflect attention from her gender. She set out to write about the difficult social system that teenagers create among themselves. Her books struck a chord with readers who saw in her characters many elements of this system that existed in their own schools and towns.

In 1967, while she was still in high school, Hinton published her first book, *The Outsiders*. The story of confrontation between rival groups of teenagers was immediately successful with critics and young readers, and it won several awards. There was some controversy about the level of violence in the novel and in her other works, but Hinton was praised for her realistic and explosive dialogue. The success of *The Outsiders* enabled Hinton to continue her education in college.

She graduated from the University of Tulsa in 1970. Her other novels for young adults include *That Was Then, This Is Now* (1971), *Rumble Fish* (1975), *Tex* (1979), and *Taming the Star Runner* (1988). *Tex*, *The Outsiders*, *Rumblefish*, and *That Was Then, This Is Now* were all made into movies.

Each of Hinton's books featured a cast of characters that suffered from society's ills. Young people alienated from their families and from their peers were seen to veer into criminal paths.

INTRODUCTION

This unit has been designed to develop students reading, writing, thinking, listening and speaking skills through exercises and activities related to *Rumble Fish* by S. E. Hinton. It includes eighteen lessons, supported by extra resource materials.

The **introductory lesson** introduces students to one main theme of the novel, the problems of delinquent youths, through a bulletin board activity. Following the introductory activity, students are given an explanation of how the activity relates to the book they are about to read.

The **reading assignments** are approximately twenty pages each; some are a little shorter while others are a little longer. Students have approximately 15 minutes of pre-reading work to do prior to each reading assignment. This pre-reading work involves reviewing the study questions for the assignment and doing some vocabulary work for 5 to 10 vocabulary words they will encounter in their reading.

The **study guide questions** are fact-based questions; students can find the answers to these questions right in the text. These questions come in two formats: short answer or multiple choice. The best use of these materials is probably to use the short answer version of the questions as study guides for students (since answers will be more complete), and to use the multiple choice version for occasional quizzes. It might be a good idea to make transparencies of your answer keys for the overhead projector.

The **vocabulary work** is intended to enrich students' vocabularies as well as to aid in the students understanding of the book. Prior to each reading assignment, students will complete a two-part worksheet for approximately 5 to 10 vocabulary words in the upcoming reading assignment. Part I focuses on students' use of general knowledge and contextual clues by giving the sentence in which the word appears in the text. Students are then to write down what they think the words mean based on the words' usage. Part II gives students dictionary definitions of the words and has them match the words to the correct definitions based on the words' contextual usage. Students should then have an understanding of the words when they meet them in the text.

After each reading assignment, students will go back and formulate answers for the study guide questions. Discussion of these questions serves as a **review** of the most important events and ideas presented in the reading assignments.

After students complete extra discussion questions, there is a **vocabulary review** lesson which pulls together all of the separate vocabulary lists for the reading assignments and gives students a review of all of the words they have studied.

Following the reading of the book, two lessons are devoted to the **extra discussion questions/writing assignments**. These questions focus on interpretation, critical analysis and personal response, employing a variety of thinking skills and adding to the students' understanding of the novel. These questions are done as a **group activity**. Using the information they have acquired so far through individual work and class discussions, students get together to further examine the text and to brainstorm ideas relating to the themes of the novel.

The group activity is followed by a **reports and discussion** session in which the groups share their ideas about the book with the entire class; thus, the entire class gets exposed to many different ideas regarding the themes and events of the book.

There are three **writing assignments** in this unit, each with the purpose of informing, persuading, or having students express personal opinions. The first assignment is to express a personal **opinion**: students will give their opinion on one of the topics dealt with in the novel (drugs, alcohol, stealing, gangs). The second assignment is to **inform:** students will write a cinquain poem about the novel. The third assignment is to **persuade:** Students will prepare a talk to give to Rusty-James to persuade him to change.

In addition, there is a **nonfiction reading assignment**. Students are required to read a piece of nonfiction related in some way to *Rumblefish*. After reading their nonfiction pieces, students will fill out a worksheet on which they answer questions regarding facts, interpretation, criticism, and personal opinions. During one class period, students make **oral presentations** about the nonfiction pieces they have read. This not only exposes all students to a wealth of information, it also gives students the opportunity to practice **public speaking**.

The **review lesson** pulls together all of the aspects of the unit. The teacher is given four or five choices of activities or games to use which all serve the same basic function of reviewing all of the information presented in the unit.

The **unit test** comes in two formats: all multiple choice-matching-true/false or with a mixture of matching, short answer, and composition. As a convenience, two different tests for each format have been included.

There are additional **support materials** included with this unit. The **unit resource section** includes suggestions for an in-class library, crossword and word search puzzles related to the novel, and extra vocabulary worksheets. There is a list of **bulletin board ideas** which gives the teacher suggestions for bulletin boards to go along with this unit. In addition, there is a list of **extra class activities** the teacher could choose from to enhance the unit or as a substitution for an exercise the teacher might feel is inappropriate for his/her class. **Answer keys** are located directly after the **reproducible student materials** throughout the unit. The student materials may be reproduced for use in the teacher's classroom without infringement of copyrights. No other portion of this unit may be reproduced without the written consent of Teacher's Pet Publications, Inc.

UNIT OBJECTIVES *Rumble Fish*

1. Through reading *Rumble Fish* students will analyze characters and their situations to better understand the themes of the novel.

2. Students will demonstrate their understanding of the text on four levels: factual, interpretive, critical, and personal.

3. Students will practice reading aloud and silently to improve their skills in each area.

4. Students will enrich their vocabularies and improve their understanding of the novel through the vocabulary lessons prepared for use in conjunction with it.

5. Students will answer questions to demonstrate their knowledge and understanding of the main events and characters in *Rumble Fish*.

6. Students will practice writing through a variety of writing assignments.

7. The writing assignments in this are geared to several purposes:
    a. To check the students' reading comprehension
    b. To make students think about the ideas presented by the novel
    c. To make students put those ideas into perspective
    d. To encourage critical and logical thinking
    e. To provide the opportunity to practice good grammar and improve students' use of the English language.

8. Students will read aloud, report, and participate in large and small group discussions to improve their public speaking and personal interaction skills.

UNIT OUTLINE - *Rumble Fish*

1 Introduction PV 1-2	2 R 1-2 ??s 1-2 Mini Lesson Flashback	3 PVR 3 Oral Reading Evaluations	4 PVR 4-5 ??s 4-5 Minilesson: Conflict	5 Quiz 1-5 Writing Assignment 1 Personal Opinion
6 PVR 6-7 Mini Lesson: Character Sketch	7 Study ??s 6-7 PVR 8-9	8 Study ??s 8-9 Writing Assignment 2 Cinquain Poem	9 Writing Conference PVR 10-12	10 Mini Lesson: Story Elements Study ??s 10-12
11 Extra Discussion ??s	12 Writing Assignment 3 Persuade	13 Group Work	14 Vocabulary Review	15 Unit Review
16 Test	17 Non-fiction Assignment	18 Movie/Audio Discussion		

Key: P = Preview Study Questions V = Prereading Vocabulary Worksheet R = Read

READING ASSIGNMENT SHEET - *Rumble Fish*

Date Assigned	Chapters Assigned	Completion Date
	1-2	
	3	
	4-5	
	6-7	
	8-9	
	10-12	

STUDY GUIDE QUESTIONS

SHORT ANSWER STUDY QUESTIONS - *Rumble Fish*

Chapters 1 & 2
1. Where was Rusty-James when the story opened?
2. Whom did he meet? What did they talk about?
3. Steve made a comment that got Rusty-James remembering something. What was Steve's comment?
4. What literary device starts at the beginning of Chapter 2?
5. What are Rusty-James's two main problems in Chapter 2?
6. How did Steve and some of the other boys feel about the fight between Rusty-James and Biff?
7. Rusty James said Steve reminded him of something. What was it?

Chapter 3
1. Where did Rusty-James go when he left Benny's?
2. What did Patty want Rusty-James to do? What was his answer?
3. What was the tension between Smokey and Rusty-James?
4. What condition was Biff in? How did Rusty-James feel about it?
5. What was it about the way Biff was fighting that upset Rusty-James the most? Why?
6. Describe the fight. Include the way it ended.
7. What had happened to the Motorcycle Boy in school? Why?
8. How old are the Motorcycle Boy and Rusty-James? What do they look like? What is their relationship?
9. What did Steve say the difference between the Motorcycle Boy and Rusty-James was?
10. How did Rusty-James feel about the Motorcycle Boy?

Chapters 4 & 5
1. Describe the scene with Coach Ryan.
2. Describe the scene with the Chevy. What did Rusty-James do, why, and what was Steve's reaction?
3. Who was Cassandra? What did she and Rusty-James talk about?
4. What was Rusty James's father's reaction to the knife wound?
5. How did Rusty-James feel about his father?
6. What rumor did his father ask Rusty-James about? What did Rusty-James tell him?

Short Answer Study Questions *Rumble Fish*

Chapters 6 & 7
1. What happened to Rusty-James at school? How did he feel about it?
2. What happened when Rusty-James saw Patty at the bus stop? How did he feel about it ?
3. Describe the scene between Rusty-James and the Motorcycle Boy in the drugstore.
4. What was it about the Motorcycle Boy that scared Rusty-James?
5. How did Rusty-James feel about the city?
6. Why didn't the Motorcycle Boy drink alcohol?
7. What happened when they went into the movie theater?
8. What did the Motorcycle Boy tell Rusty-James while they were walking along? How did Rusty-James react to the news?

Chapters 8 & 9
1. How did Rusty-James describe the feeling when the black guy hit him?
2. How was Rusty-James saved?
3. What did the Motorcycle Boy say about the gangs?
4. The Motorcycle Boy said Rusty-James had one vice. What was it?
5. What scared Steve and Rusty-James about the Motorcycle Boy?
6. Describe what happened at Steve's house.
7. What did Rusty-James tell Steve he wanted the two of them to do? What was Steve's reply?
8. How did Rusty-James react to Steve's answer?
9. What did Steve say next to Rusty-James? How did Rusty-James react? How did the discussion end?

Chapters 10 - 12
1. Why did Rusty-James say he liked telling about the things that happened?
2. Describe the scene between Smokey and Rusty-James at Benny's.
3. Why did Smokey say he would be president if there were still gangs? How did Rusty-James react?
4. Where was the Motorcycle Boy, and what was he doing? What did he say to Rusty-James?
5. The Motorcycle Boy said he was sorry about something. What was it?
6. Describe the discussion between Rusty-James and his father about his mother and the Motorcycle Boy.
7. Where did Rusty-James and the Motorcycle Boy go that night? What happened?
8. What happened to Rusty-James?
9. Was Rusty-James planning to meet Steve for dinner? What was his reason?

ANSWER KEY: SHORT ANSWER STUDY QUESTIONS *Rumble Fish*

Chapters 1 & 2

1. Where was Rusty-James when the story opened?
    He was on a beach in an unnamed location.

2. Whom did he meet? What did they talk about?
    He met his old friend, Steve Hays. They talked about the old neighborhood, and how they both got to this beach town. Steve wanted them and their girl friends to meet for dinner that evening.

3. Steve made a comment that got Rusty-James remembering something. What was Steve's comment?
    He asked Rusty-James if he realized he looks like someone else. That jogged Rusty's memory.

4. What literary device starts at the beginning of Chapter 2?
    From Chapter Two through Chapter Eleven, the novel is told in flashback.

5. What are Rusty-James's two main problems in Chapter 2?
    Biff Wilcox wants to fight him, and the Motorcycle Boy has not returned from his trip. Rusty-James is not sure if he will come back at all.

6. How did Steve and some of the other boys feel about the fight between Rusty-James and Biff?
    They were concerned that it would turn into a gang fight, and there had not been any gangs around for a long time.

7. Rusty James said Steve reminded him of something. What was it?
    He said Steve reminded him of a rabbit.

Chapter 3

1. Where did Rusty-James go when he left Benny's?
    He went to his girlfriend, Patty's, house.

2. What did Patty want Rusty-James to do? What was his answer?
    She wanted him to stop fighting. He said he didn't do it all the time, it was just this once, and it wasn't his fault.

3. What was the tension between Smokey and Rusty-James?
    Smokey would have been the number one tough cat if it were not for Rusty-James.

4. What condition was Biff in? How did Rusty-James feel about it?
    Biff was doped up. Rusty-James didn't like it. He said guys who fought while on dope could not tell if they had been killed.

5. What was it about the way Biff was fighting that upset Rusty-James the most? Why?
    Rusty-James was upset that Biff had a knife and had not told him about it before the fight. According to Rusty-James, Biff had violated the rules by not telling him.

6. Describe the fight. Include the way it ended.
    Biff had a knife. Someone gave Rusty-James a bicycle chain. Rusty-James was able to get the knife away from Biff. The Motorcycle Boy arrived and Rusty got distracted. Biff cut him along the side. The Motorcycle Boy broke Biff's wrist. That ended the fight.

7. What had happened to the Motorcycle Boy in school? Why?
    He had been expelled because he had perfect semester test grades.

8. How old are the Motorcycle Boy and Rusty-James? What do they look like? What is their relationship?
    They are brothers. The Motorcycle Boy is seventeen, and Rusty-James is fourteen. They both had dark red/black hair and brown eyes. Rusty-James said the Motorcycle Boy looked like a panther and he looked like a tough kid who was too big for his age.

9. What did Steve say the difference between the Motorcycle Boy and Rusty-James was?
    Steve said he could tell what Rusty-James was thinking, but not what the Motorcycle Boy was thinking.

10. How did Rusty-James feel about the Motorcycle Boy?
    He thought the Motorcycle Boy was "the coolest person in the world." He wanted to be just like him.

Chapters 4 & 5
1. Describe the scene with Coach Ryan.
    The coach offered Rusty-James five dollars to beat up another student who was giving him trouble in class. Rusty-James said he couldn't because of the knife wound. The coach told Rusty-James to let him know when the wound was healed.

2. Describe the scene with the Chevy. What did Rusty-James do, why, and what was Steve's reaction?
    Rusty-James wanted some quick money. He saw a Chevy with mag wheels and decided to steal them. Steve was upset because he didn't steal. As they were taking off the fourth

hubcap, three guys came from the apartment house and started chasing them. Steve threw down the hubcaps. Rusty-James ran into an apartment house and up onto the roof. He jumped across to the next roof. Steve was afraid to jump, but finally did it. After they got across, Steve told Rusty-James he should not have stolen the hubcaps, but Rusty-James ignored him. Then he passed out. Steve went into the building and got help, but by the time he and the woman he found got back to the roof, Rusty-James was awake again. On their way home, Steve started crying.
Rusty-James thought he was worried about his mother.

3. Who was Cassandra? What did she and Rusty-James talk about?
Cassandra had been a student teacher at the high school, and had become romantically interested in the Motorcycle Boy. She had been visiting him, and met Rusty-James on the steps as she was leaving his apartment. He told her the Motorcycle Boy didn't like her. She said he didn't like her now, and showed Rusty-James the heroin tracks on her arms. She said she was not hooked, but had done it because she thought the Motorcycle Boy was gone for good.

4. What was Rusty James's father's reaction to the knife wound?
He said his sons led interesting lives. Then he gave Rusty-James ten dollars.

5. How did Rusty-James feel about his father?
He wasn't sure exactly how he felt. They got along okay, but didn't talk much. Rusty-James found it hard to respect his father, because he didn't do any work. He thought his father liked him more than he liked the Motorcycle Boy.

6. What rumor did his father ask Rusty-James about? What did Rusty-James tell him?
His father said there was a rumor that a policeman was out to get one of the boys. He asked which one. Rusty-James said it was both of them, but mostly the Motorcycle Boy.

Chapters 6 & 7
1. What happened to Rusty-James at school? How did he feel about it?
He was expelled. The guidance counselor told him he would be transferred to Cleveland High School. Rusty-James didn't want to go there, because Biff and his friends ran the school. The counselor said the alternative was the Youth Detention Center. Rusty-James decided to take his chances and stay out of school altogether until the Detention Center caught up with him. He thought he had a few weeks to figure out what to do.

2. What happened when Rusty-James saw Patty at the bus stop? How did he feel about it?
Patty got off the bus and ignored him. Then she said she was breaking up with him because he had been with another girl at the lake. Rusty-James didn't understand what his

being with a girl at the lake had to do with him and Patty. He wondered if he was going to cry, but he felt better in a little while.

3. Describe the scene between Rusty-James and the Motorcycle Boy in the drugstore.
   The Motorcycle Boy was looking at a magazine. There was a picture of him that a photographer in California had taken. Rusty-James wanted to tell everyone, but the Motorcycle Boy didn't want him to.

4. What was it about the Motorcycle Boy that scared Rusty-James?
   It scared Rusty-James when the Motorcycle Boy smiled.

5. How did Rusty-James feel about the city?
   He liked it. He wished they lived in the city. He liked the lights, the colors, and the energy.

6. Why didn't the Motorcycle Boy drink alcohol?
   He liked control.

7. What happened when they went into the movie theater?
   Steve was shocked by what he saw on the screen. He left and went to the bathroom. When he didn't come back into the theater, the Motorcycle Boy and Rusty-James left to find him. Then they all left the theater.

8. What did the Motorcycle Boy tell Rusty-James while they were walking along? How did Rusty-James react to the news?
   He said he saw their mother in California. She wanted him to stay there with her. Rusty-James was upset because the Motorcycle Boy had not told him about it when he got back from California.

Chapters 8 & 9

1. How did Rusty-James describe the feeling when the black guy hit him?
   He said he was floating up in the air looking down at the others. It was like watching a movie. He heard the black guy say, "Killed him. Better get this one too." Then he saw his body laying on the alley floor. He knew he had to get back to his body, and a minute later he realized his head was hurting.

2. How was Rusty-James saved?
   The Motorcycle Boy came along and stopped the attack.

3. What did the Motorcycle Boy say about the gangs?
   He said it was fun at first, but then it got boring. He got the credit for ending the rumbles

because everyone knew he thought they were boring. They would have ended anyway, because too many of the members were doing dope.

4. The Motorcycle Boy said Rusty-James had one vice. What was it?
   The Motorcycle Boy said loyalty was his only vice.

5. What scared Steve and Rusty-James about the Motorcycle Boy?
   He didn't belong anywhere, and didn't want to.

6. Describe what happened at Steve's house.
   Rusty-James went to Steve's house after he left the clinic. He had never been there before. Steve's father had beaten him up for getting home so late. Steve defended his father to Rusty-James. He asked Rusty-James to say he got beat up during their confrontation with the two boys in the city.

7. What did Rusty-James tell Steve he wanted the two of them to do? What was Steve's reply?
   Rusty-James wanted to follow the Motorcycle Boy around for a few days. Steve said he would not do it. He told Rusty-James to ask B. J. or Smokey. Rusty-James said they would laugh at him. Steve said that they didn't know the Motorcycle Boy was nuts. Rusty-James got very angry at that and knocked him against the wall.

8. How did Rusty-James react to Steve's answer?
   He felt like crying, but he didn't.

9. What did Steve say next to Rusty-James? How did Rusty-James react? How did the discussion end?
   He said he had tried to help him, but he was like a ball in a pinball machine. He never thought about anything. Steve said he could not keep on thinking for himself and Rusty-James, too. Rusty-James didn't understand what Steve meant. He asked Steve why he thought the Motorcycle Boy was cool. Steve said it was because he was like someone out of a book. Steve told Rusty-James to let go of the Motorcycle Boy, or he would not believe in anything. Rusty-James said he believed everything. Steve said he was sorry. Rusty-James left, and that was the last time they saw each other.

Chapters 10-12

1. Why did Rusty-James say he liked telling about the things that happened?
   He said it took the scare out, and made it more like an exciting movie.

2. Describe the scene between Smokey and Rusty-James at Benny's.
   Patty came into Benny's. Smokey came in and sat with her. Rusty-James asked Smokey

to step outside, and Smokey said he would not fight. They went outside and Rusty-James asked Smokey if he had planned for the news about the party to get back to Patty. Smokey said he did. Rusty-James said it was a smart thing to do, that he would not have thought of it.

3. Why did Smokey say he would be president if there were still gangs? How did Rusty-James react?
   No one would want to follow Rusty-James into a fight, because he would get them killed. Rusty-James agreed.

4. Where was the Motorcycle Boy, and what was he doing? What did he say to Rusty-James?
   He was in the pet store looking a the Siamese fighting fish. He said he wondered if they would try to kill each other if they were in the river.

5. The Motorcycle Boy said he was sorry about something. What was it?
   He was sorry he could not see the colors of the fish.

6. Describe the discussion between Rusty-James and his father about his mother and the Motorcycle Boy.
   Rusty-James asked his father if his mother was nuts. His father said she had married him for fun, and when the fun stopped she left. He said she had a different view of the world. His father said his mother was not crazy, and neither was the Motorcycle Boy. The Motorcycle Boy was born in the wrong era. He had the ability to do whatever he wanted, but didn't want to do anything.

7. Where did Rusty-James and the Motorcycle Boy go that night? What happened?
   The Motorcycle Boy broke into the pet store, and Rusty-James was with him. The Motorcycle Boy let out all the animals. He took the fighting fish to the river. On the way there, the police got them. The Motorcycle Boy was shot and killed by Patterson, the policeman who had said he would get them.

8. What happened to Rusty-James?
   He was running after the Motorcycle Boy and heard the shots. He saw the police turn the Motorcycle Boy over. He was thrown up against the police car and frisked. He noticed that he could not see the color in the flashing light. He also could not hear. He slammed his fists through the police car window and slashed his wrists on the glass. The police took him to the hospital.

9. Was Rusty-James planning to meet Steve for dinner? What was his reason?
   No, he was not planning to meet Steve for dinner. He thought if he did not see Steve, he could start forgetting again.

MULTIPLE CHOICE STUDY/QUIZ QUESTIONS *Rumble Fish*

Chapters 1 & 2

1. Where was Rusty-James when the story opened?
    A. He was in a hospital.
    B. He was in school.
    C. He was on a beach.
    D. He was in a prison.

2. How did Rusty-James know Steve Hays?
    A. Steve was his roommate at the reformatory.
    B. Steve was his former P. E. teacher.
    C. Steve worked at the same restaurant as Rusty-James.
    D. Steve was his best friend from the old neighborhood.

3. True or False: Steve asked Rusty-James if he realized he looks like someone else. That jogged Rusty's memory.
    A. True
    B. False

4. What literary device starts at the beginning of Chapter 2 and goes through Chapter 11?
    A. metaphor
    B. flashback
    C. hyperbole
    D. personification

5. What are Rusty-James's two main problems in Chapter 2?
    A. He is competing with the Motorcycle Boy to become the new gang leader, and the girl he likes doesn't like him.
    B. He is failing in school and his mother has just left him and his brother alone and gone off with another man.
    C. Biff Wilcox wants to fight him, and the Motorcycle Boy has not returned from his trip.
    D. His father has been missing for a week, and he doesn't have any money to buy food or pay the rent.

6. True or False: Steve and the others were glad Rusty-James was going to fight. They said there had not been enough action lately.
    A. True
    B. False

Multiple Choice Questions *Rumble Fish*

7. Rusty James said Steve reminded him of something. What was it?
    A. He said Steve reminded him of a rabbit.
    B. He said Steve reminded him of a turtle.
    C. He said Steve reminded him of a weasel.
    D. He said Steve reminded him of a panther.

Multiple Choice Questions *Rumble Fish*

Chapter 3

1. Where did Rusty-James go when he left Benny's?
    A. He went to the drugstore to look at the magazines.
    B. He went to his girlfriend, Patty's, house.
    C. He went home.
    D. He went to the gym to work out.

2. True or False: Rusty-James promised Patty that he would not fight with Biff.
    A. True
    B. False

3. True or False: Smokey would have been the number one tough cat if it were not for Rusty-James.
    A. True
    B. False

4. What condition was Biff in? How did Rusty-James feel about it?
    A. Biff had been taking karate lessons and was in good shape. Rusty-James was scared.
    B. Biff was drunk. Rusty-James was glad, because it made the fight easier for him.
    C. Biff was angry because his girlfriend had just broken up with him. Rusty-James said it was dangerous to fight a guy who was mad about a girl.
    D. Biff was doped up. Rusty-James didn't like it because guys on dope could not tell if they had been killed.

5. Rusty-James was upset that Biff was violating the rules. How was Biff doing this?
    A. Biff had a knife and had not told him about it before the fight.
    B. Biff had brought more friends than he said he would, so the sides were not even.
    C. Biff had a gun, and the gangs had agreed not to use guns.
    D. Biff got to the empty lot early and booby-trapped it.

6. Which of the following did **not** happen during the fight?
    A. Someone gave Rusty-James a bicycle chain.
    B. Someone called the police and they broke up the fight.
    C. Biff cut Rusty-James along the side.
    D. The Motorcycle Boy broke Biff's wrist.

Multiple Choice Questions *Rumble Fish*

7. What had happened to the Motorcycle Boy in school? Why?
   A. He had to repeat his senior year because he had been absent too often.
   B. He was offered a chance to go to the technical school to study auto mechanics but he turned it down because he didn't want to work.
   C. He had been expelled because he had perfect semester test grades.
   D. He had skipped two grades when he was younger. Now he was too young to get a job, although he was old enough to graduate from high school.

8. Which of the following statements about the Motorcycle Boy and Rusty-James is true?
   A. They are cousins.
   B. The Motorcycle Boy is nineteen and Rusty-James is sixteen.
   C. They both have blonde hair and green eyes.
   D. Rusty-James said the Motorcycle Boy looked like a panther.

9. What did Steve say the difference between the Motorcycle Boy and Rusty-James was?
   A. He said the Motorcycle Boy acted, but Rusty-James only bragged.
   B. He said Rusty-James cared about people, but the Motorcycle Boy didn't.
   C. He could tell what Rusty-James was thinking, but not what the Motorcycle Boy was thinking.
   D. He said the Motorcycle Boy was tough, but Rusty-James only acted tough.

10. How did Rusty-James feel about the Motorcycle Boy?
    A. He thought the Motorcycle Boy was "the coolest person in the world." He wanted to be just like him.
    B. He was jealous because the Motorcycle Boy got all of the attention.
    C. He thought the Motorcycle Boy was nuts, and didn't like to be around him.
    D. He thought the Motorcycle Boy acted stupid.

Multiple Choice Questions *Rumble Fish*

Chapters 4 & 5

1. True or False: Coach Ryan asked Rusty-James to beat up another student who was giving him trouble in class. He said he would fail Rusty-James if he did not beat the boy up.
    A. True
    B. False

2. Which of the following did not happen in the scene with the Chevy?
    A. Rusty-James took the mag wheels off the car.
    B. They jumped from one roof to another to get away from the guys who were chasing them.
    C. After they got across, Steve told Rusty-James he should not have stolen the hubcaps, but Rusty-James ignored him.
    D. On the way home, Steve said he would report Rusty-James to the police if he ever tried to steal again.

3. Who was Cassandra?
    A. She was the boys' mother.
    B. She was a member of the girls' gang. She had a crush on Rusty-James, and wanted to steal him away from his girlfriend.
    C. She had been a student teacher at the high school, and had become romantically interested in the Motorcycle Boy.
    D. She was a writer who was interested in doing a book about gangs. She was living in the neighborhood to get to know the teenagers.

4. What was Rusty James's father's reaction to the knife wound?
    A. He was very upset. He offered to take Rusty-James to the emergency room.
    B. He told Rusty-James it was his own fault for getting into trouble.
    C. He said his sons led interesting lives. Then he gave Rusty-James ten dollars.
    D. He told Rusty-James if he got into another fight he would be put out of the apartment.

5. How did Rusty-James feel about his father?
    A. Rusty-James found it hard to respect his father, because he didn't do any work.
    B. Rusty-James hated his father. He blamed him for losing his mother.
    C. Rusty-James loved his father and felt sorry for him.
    D. Rusty-James didn't care about his father at all.

Multiple Choice Questions *Rumble Fish*

6. Which statement is true?
    A. Rusty-James thought his father liked the Motorcycle Boy the best.
    B. Rusty-James thought his father was crazy.
    C. Rusty-James thought his father liked him better than the Motorcycle Boy.
    D. Rusty-James thought his father was still in love with their mother.

7. What rumor did his father ask Rusty-James about?
    A. He said there was a rumor that Rusty-James had robbed a liquor store.
    B. He said there was a rumor that the boys had started a new gang.
    C. He said there was a rumor that the Motorcycle Boy was moving to California.
    D. He said there was a rumor that a policeman was out to get one of the boys.

Multiple Choice Questions *Rumble Fish*

<u>Chapters 6 & 7</u>

1. True or False: Rusty-James didn't want to go to Cleveland High because it was on the other side of the city and he was afraid he would not have the money for bus fare.
    A. True
    B. False

2. What happened when Rusty-James saw Patty at the bus stop?
    A. She told him she loved him.
    B. She hit him and broke his nose.
    C. She broke up with him.
    D. She invited him to go home with her.

3. What was the Motorcycle Boy doing in the drugstore?
    A. He was looking at a map of California.
    B. He was sitting at the soda fountain having a burger and milkshake.
    C. He was talking with the owner.
    D. He was looking at a magazine that had his picture in it.

4. What was it about the Motorcycle Boy that scared Rusty-James?
    A. It scared Rusty-James when the Motorcycle Boy smiled.
    B. It scared Rusty-James when the Motorcycle Boy yelled.
    C. It scared Rusty-James when the Motorcycle Boy cried.
    D. It scared Rusty-James when the Motorcycle Boy sang.

5. True or False: Rusty-James liked the lights, colors, and energy of the city.
    A. True
    B. False

6. Why didn't the Motorcycle Boy drink alcohol?
    A. He could not afford to buy it.
    B. He didn't like the feeling of a hangover.
    C. He didn't want to turn out like his father.
    D. He liked control.

Multiple Choice Questions *Rumble Fish*

7. How did Steve react to the movie?
    A. He liked it and wanted to stay for another show.
    B. He was shocked by what he saw. He left and went to the bathroom.
    C. He thought it was funny and laughed all through the movie.
    D. He was angry at Rusty-James for bringing him. He demanded that they all leave.

8. What did the Motorcycle Boy tell Rusty-James while they were walking along?
    A. He said their mother was dead.
    B. He said their parents had never been married.
    C. He said he saw their mother in California.
    D. He said he was planning to move to California permanently.

9. True or False: Rusty-James was upset because the Motorcycle Boy had not told him about it when he got back from California.
    A. True
    B. False

Multiple Choice Questions *Rumble Fish*

<u>Chapters 8 & 9</u>

1. Which of the following is **not** part of the way Rusty-James described the attack on him?
    A. The two guys asked for money.
    B. Rusty-James said he was floating up in the air looking down at the others.
    C. He heard the black guy say, "Killed him. Better get this one too."
    D. He felt someone on the ground pull his mind back into his body.

2. How was Rusty-James saved?
    A. Steve grabbed the one guy's club and hit him. The other guy ran away.
    B. A police officer heard the fight and broke it up.
    C. The attackers got scared when they thought they killed him and they left.
    D. The Motorcycle Boy came along and stopped the attack.

3. The Motorcycle Boy said it was fun at first, but then it got boring. What was he talking about?
    A. He was talking about dating Cassandra.
    B. He was talking about riding a motorcycle.
    C. He was talking about the gangs.
    D. He was talking about his life.

4. The Motorcycle Boy said the gangs would have ended. Why?
    A. The police were cracking down.
    B. There were not enough younger boys to keep them going.
    C. Too many of the members were doing dope.
    D. The adults had started a Neighborhood Watch program that stopped the gangs.

5. The Motorcycle Boy said Rusty-James had one vice. What was it?
    A. The Motorcycle Boy said jealousy was his only vice.
    B. The Motorcycle Boy said loyalty was his only vice.
    C. The Motorcycle Boy said honesty was his only vice.
    D. The Motorcycle Boy said carelessness was his only vice.

6. What scared Steve and Rusty-James about the Motorcycle Boy?
    A. He didn't belong anywhere, and didn't want to.
    B. He said he had a gun and was going to use it soon.
    C. They thought he was going to go blind and deaf.
    D. They thought he was going to leave for good and forget about them.

Multiple Choice Questions *Rumble Fish*

7. What did Rusty-James discover when he got to Steve's house?
    A. Steve's family was moving that day.
    B. Steve was grounded for a month.
    C. Steve's mother had died while he was out with Rusty-James.
    D. Steve's father had beaten him up for getting home so late.

8. What did Rusty-James tell Steve he wanted the two of them to do?
    A. Rusty-James wanted the two of them to get an apartment together.
    B. Rusty-James wanted to follow the Motorcycle Boy around for a few days.
    C. Rusty-James wanted Steve to transfer to Cleveland High with him.
    D. Rusty-James wanted Steve to help him rob the drugstore.

9. What was Steve's reply?
    A. He said yes.
    B. He said no.

10. How did Steve describe Rusty-James?
    A. He was like a ball in a pinball machine.
    B. He was like a weed in a patch of flowers.
    C. He was like a salmon swimming against the tide.
    D. He was like a lost puppy.

11. Why did Steve think the Motorcycle Boy was cool?
    A. He wore a leather jacket and smoked cigarettes.
    B. He was not afraid of anyone.
    C. He was like someone out of a book.
    D. He had girls chasing him all of the time.

Multiple Choice Questions *Rumble Fish*

Chapters 10-12

1. Why did Rusty-James say he liked telling about the things that happened?
    A. He said it took the scare out, and made it more like an exciting movie.
    B. He liked to have people pay attention to him.
    C. He wanted them to think he was tougher than the Motorcycle Boy.
    D. It made his life seem more exciting than it was.

2. True or False: Rusty-James challenged Smokey to a fight. Smokey agreed, and the winner would get Patty.
    A. True
    B. False

3. Who said he would be president if there were still gangs?
    A. Biff
    B. Rusty-James
    C. Smokey
    D. the Motorcycle Boy

4. What did the Motorcycle Boy say to Rusty-James in the pet store?
    A. He wondered if Mr. Dobson would ever be able to sell the parrot.
    B. He wondered if the Siamese fighting fish would kill each other in the river.
    C. He wanted to buy all of the animals.
    D. He wanted to get a job working there with Mr. Dobson.

5. The Motorcycle Boy said he was sorry about something. What was it?
    A. He was sorry he could not see the colors of the fish.
    B. He was sorry he could not take all of the animals home with him.
    C. He was sorry the animals did not have humans to love them.
    D. He was sorry he had ever come back from California.

6. Rusty-James asked his father about his mother. Which of the following statements was **not** part of his father's answer?
    A. His father said she had married him for fun, and when the fun stopped she left.
    B. His father said his mother was crazy.
    C. He said she had a different view of the world
    D. He said he married her to set a precedent.

Multiple Choice Questions *Rumble Fish*

7. What did their father say about the Motorcycle Boy?
    A. The Motorcycle Boy would make a good Greek god.
    B. The Motorcycle Boy would never amount to anything because he was lazy.
    C. The Motorcycle Boy was just like their mother.
    D. The Motorcycle Boy was born in the wrong era.

8. Where did Rusty-James and the Motorcycle Boy go that night?
    A. They went back to the city. They found the guys who had attacked Rusty-James, and beat them up.
    B. They broke into the pet store. The Motorcycle Boy let out all the animals. He took the fighting fish to the river.
    C. They went to the school and broke all of the windows by throwing rocks.
    D. They went to a party and met two girls. They got into a fight when another boy said he was the one girl's boyfriend.

9. True or False: The Motorcycle Boy was shot and killed by Patterson, the policeman who had said he would get them.
    A. True
    B. False

10. Which of the following did **not** happen to Rusty-James?
    A. He was thrown up against the police car and searched.
    B. He attacked Patterson with a piece of broken glass.
    C. He noticed that he could not see the color in the flashing light. He also could not hear.
    D. The police took him to the hospital.

11. Was Rusty-James planning to meet Steve for dinner? What was his reason?
    A. Yes. He thought it would be good for him to connect with someone from his past who meant a lot to him.
    B. No. He did not want anyone he knew to find out what he used to be like.
    C. No. He thought if he did not see Steve, he could start forgetting again.
    D. Yes. He thought Steve might be able to help him remember some of the good times they had.

STUDENT ANSWER SHEET-MULTIPLE CHOICE/QUIZ QUESTIONS *Rumble Fish*

Chapters 1 & 2
1.
2.
3.
4.
5.
6.
7.
8.
9.
10.

Chapter 3
1.
2.
3.
4.
5.
6.
7.
8.
9.
10.

Chapters 4 & 5
1.
2.
3.
4.
5.
6.
7.
8.
9.
10.

Chapters 6 & 7
1.
2.
3.
4.
5.
6.
7.
8.
9.
10.

Chapters 8 & 9
1.
2.
3.
4.
5.
6.
7.
8.
9.
10.

Chapters 10-12
1.
2.
3.
4.
5.
6.
7.
8.
9.
10.

ANSWER KEY-MULTIPLE CHOICE/QUIZ QUESTIONS *Rumble Fish*

<u>Chapters 1 & 2</u>
1. C
2. D
3. A True
4. B
5. C
6. B False
7. A

<u>Chapter 3</u>
1. B
2. B False
3. A True
4. D
5. A
6. B
7. C
8. D
9. C
10. A

<u>Chapters 4 & 5</u>
1. B False
2. D
3. C
4. C
5. A
6. C
7. D

<u>Chapters 6 & 7</u>
1. B False
2. C
3. D
4. A
5. A True
6. D
7. B
8. C
9. A True

<u>Chapters 8 & 9</u>
1. D
2. D
3. C
4. C
5. B
6. A
7. D
8. B
9. B
10. A
11. C

<u>Chapters 10-12</u>
1. A
2. B False
3. C
4. B
5. A
6. B
7. D
8. B
9. A True
10. B
11. C

VOCABULARY WORKSHEETS

Vocabulary Worksheets *Rumble Fish*

Chapters 1 & 2
Part I: Using Prior Knowledge and Context Clues
Below are the sentences in which the vocabulary words appear in the text. Read the sentence. Use any clues you can find in the sentence combined with your prior knowledge, and write what you think the underlined words mean on the lines provided.

1. "They put me in *solitary* once," I said, because Steve seemed to be waiting for something.

   _____

2. "Just one," I said. I like to keep things simple, and God knows even one can get *complicated* enough.

   _____

3. "He wants you to meet him in the *vacant* lot behind the pet store."

   _____

4. Steve was always *cautious* about things.

   _____

5. "But even back when we was rumblin', we never fought Biff's gang. They was *allies*."

   _____

6. He'd *pestered* me once before when he shouldn't of and I'd punched the wind out of him.

   _____

Part II: Determining the Meaning Match the vocabulary words to their dictionary definitions.

1.	solitary	A.	empty
2.	complicated	B.	supporters; partners
3.	vacant	C.	alone
4.	cautious	D.	careful
5.	pestered	E.	bothered; annoyed
6.	allies	F.	difficult; involved

Vocabulary Worksheets *Rumble Fish*

Chapter 3
Part I: Using Prior Knowledge and Context Clues
Below are the sentences in which the vocabulary words appear in the text. Read the sentence. Use any clues you can find in the sentence combined with your prior knowledge, and write what you think the underlined words mean on the lines provided.

1. We had a funny kind of *tension* between us anyway.

   _____

2. "If you think this is gonna turn out to be a *rumble*, you're crazy."

   _____

3. He said it *sarcastic*. They never could understand why I let Steve hang around.

   _____

4. Gradually I started to calm down, the red *tinge* to everything went away, I could hear everyone screaming and yelling.

   _____

5. Biff stood a few feet away from me, laughing like a *maniac.*

   _____

6. After a while I was kind of *dozing* off and on.

   _____

Part II: Determining the Meaning Match the vocabulary words to their dictionary definitions.
1. tension   A. napping
2. rumble   B. madman; lunatic
3. sarcastic   C. small amount of color
4. tinge   D. mocking
5. maniac   E. a gang fight
6. dozing   F. anxiety; unease

Vocabulary Worksheets *Rumble Fish*

<u>Chapters 4 & 5</u>
Part I: Using Prior Knowledge and Context Clues
Below are the sentences in which the vocabulary words appear in the text. Read the sentence. Use any clues you can find in the sentence combined with your prior knowledge, and write what you think the underlined words mean on the lines provided.

1. He was mouthy just to get on people's nerves. A real *obnoxious* kid.

   _____

2. I did a lot of *scrounging* around.

   _____

3. So when I spotted a set of real cool *simulated* mags on a late model Chevy, I saw a quick way to make twenty bucks.

   _____

4. She had always seemed stuck-up, like she thought her and the Motorcycle Boy belonged to some *superelite* club or something.

   _____

5. She wasn't so *sassy* now.

   _____

Part II: Determining the Meaning Match the vocabulary words to their dictionary definitions.

   1. obnoxious   A. searching for what one can find
   2. scrounging   B. high-fashion
   3. simulated   C. offensive; annoying
   4. superelite   D. lively
   5. sassy   E. imitation

Vocabulary Worksheets *Rumble Fish*

<u>Chapters 6 & 7</u>
Part I: Using Prior Knowledge and Context Clues
Below are the sentences in which the vocabulary words appear in the text. Read the sentence. Use any clues you can find in the sentence combined with your prior knowledge, and write what you think the underlined words mean on the lines provided.

1. "We have decided that we can no longer *tolerate* your kind of behavior."

   _____

2. "The *alternative* is the Youth Detention Center."

   _____

3. Then, when she went *stalking* on down the street, her hair bouncing on her shoulders, her head up. a tough, sweet little chick, I thought of how I wouldn't be going over to her house to watch TV anymore.

   _____

4. "I'd just as soon stay a neighborhood *novelty*, if it's all the same to you."

   _____

5. I really thought that was funny, and I laughed, but Steve glared at him--a rabbit *scowling* at a panther.

   _____

6. "She *abandoned* me eventually, and they took me back to the old man."

   _____

7. "She abandoned me *eventually*, and they took me back to the old man."

   _____

Vocabulary Worksheets *Rumble Fish*

8. Steve looked at me *dazedly* and said, "Is this real? Is this real?" and seemed terrified when he realized he wasn't dreaming.

   _____

9. Everything was *throbbing* with noise and music and energy.

   _____

Part II: Determining the Meaning Match the vocabulary words to their dictionary definitions.

1. tolerate   A. confused
2. alternative   B. looking angry by lowering the eyebrows
3. stalking   C. choice
4. novelty   D. aching
5. scowling   E. finally
6. abandoned   F. new and unusual thing
7. eventually   G. deserted; left
8. dazedly   H. walking in an angry manner
9. throbbing   I. permit; endure

Vocabulary Worksheets *Rumble Fish*

<u>Chapters 8 & 9</u>
Part I: Using Prior Knowledge and Context Clues
Below are the sentences in which the vocabulary words appear in the text. Read the sentence. Use any clues you can find in the sentence combined with your prior knowledge, and write what you think the underlined words mean on the lines provided.

1. That was when the black guy *clipped* me across the head.

   _____

2. A harsh, breathing kind of sound kept *rasping* in my ears, until the Motorcycle Boy said, "Will you stop that crying?" and Steve said, "Will you go to hell?"

   _____

3. "Even the most *primitive* societies have an innate respect for the insane," the Motorcycle Boy answered.

   _____

4. "Even the most primitive societies have an *innate* respect for the insane," the Motorcycle Boy answered.

   _____

5. And since getting *clobbered*, everything even looked funny, like I was seeing things through *distorted* glass.

   _____

Part II: Determining the Meaning Match the vocabulary words to their dictionary definitions.

1. clipped   A. inherited; inborn
2. rasping   B. deformed; twisted out of shape
3. primitive   C. a harsh, grating sound
4. innate   D. uncivilized; simple
5. distorted   E. hit with a sharp blow

Vocabulary Worksheets *Rumble Fish*

Chapters 10, 11, 12
Part I: Using Prior Knowledge and Context Clues
Below are the sentences in which the vocabulary words appear in the text. Read the sentence. Use any clues you can find in the sentence combined with your prior knowledge, and write what you think the underlined words mean on the lines provided.

1. "Our marriage was a classic example of a preacher marrying an *atheist,* thinking to make a convert, and instead ending up doubting his own faith."

   ___

2. "I married her, thinking to set a *precedent*."

   ___

3. "An *acute* perception does not make you crazy."

   ___

4. "An acute *perception* does not make you crazy."

   ___

5. "Neither, *contrary* to popular belief, is your brother."

   ___

6. "He is merely *miscast* in a play."

   ___

7. "He would have made a perfect knight, in a different century, or a very good *pagan* prince in a time of heroes."

   ___

Vocabulary Worksheets *Rumble Fish*

8. "He was born in the wrong *era*, on the wrong side of the river, with the ability to do anything and finding nothing he wants to do."

_____

Part II: Determining the Meaning   Match the vocabulary words to their dictionary definitions.

1. atheist
2. precedent
3. acute
4. perception
5. contrary
6. miscast
7. pagan
8. era

A. put in an unsuitable role
B. insight
C. a period of time
D. intense
E. example for future actions
F. a person who worships many gods
G. one who does not believe in God
H. opposite

ANSWER KEY-PREREADING VOCABULARY WORKSHEETS *Rumble Fish*

Chapters 1 & 2
1. C
2. F
3. A
4. D
5. E
6. B

Chapter 3
1. F
2. E
3. D
4. C
5. B
6. A

Chapters 4 & 5
1. C
2. A
3. E
4. B
5. D

Chapters 6 & 7
1. I
2. C
3. H
4. F
5. B
6. G
7. E
8. A
9. D

Chapters 8 & 9
1. E
2. C
3. D
4. A
5. B

Chapters 10-12
1. G
2. E
3. D
4. B
5. H
6. A
7. F
8. C

DAILY LESSONS

LESSON ONE

Student Objectives
1. To preview the *Rumble Fish* Unit
2. To receive books and other related materials (study guides, reading assignment)
3. To relate prior knowledge to the new material
4. To become familiar with the vocabulary for Chapters 1&2
5. To preview the study questions for Chapters 1&2

Activity #1

Before beginning the book, make a bulletin board display of city areas, such as downtown buildings, houses and apartments close together, and the city lights at night. Also include pictures of teenagers in leather jackets and blue jeans, and tough looking, gang-like teens. Ask students to describe what they see.

Activity #2

Distribute the materials students will use in this unit. Explain in detail how students are to use these materials.

Study Guides Students should preview the study guide questions before each reading assignment to get a feeling for which events and ideas are important in that section. After reading the section, students will (as a class or individually) answer the questions to review the important events and ideas from that section of the book. Students should keep the study guides as study materials for the unit test.

Reading Assignment Sheet You need to fill in the reading assignment sheet to let students know when their reading has to be completed. You can either write the assignment sheet on a side blackboard or bulletin board and leave it there for students to see each day, or you can duplicate copies for each student to have. In either case, you should advise students to become very familiar with the reading assignments so they know what is expected of them.

Unit Outline You may find it helpful to distribute copies of the Unit Outline to your students so they can keep track of upcoming lessons and assignments. You may also want to post a copy of the Unit Outline on a bulletin board and cross off each lesson as you complete it.

Extra Activities Center The Unit Resource portion of this unit contains suggestions for a library of related books and articles in your classroom as well as crossword and word search puzzles. Make an extra activities center in your room where you will keep these materials for students to use. Bring the books and articles in from the library and keep several copies of the puzzles on hand. Explain to students that these materials are available for students to use when they finish reading assignments or other class work early.

<u>Books</u> Each school has its own rules and regulations regarding student use of school books. Advise students of the procedures that are normal for your school.

<u>Notebook or Unit Folder</u> You may want the students to keep all of their worksheets, notes, and other papers for the unit together in a binder or notebook. During the first class meeting, tell them how you want them to arrange the folder. Make divider pages for vocabulary worksheets, prereading study guide questions, review activities, notes, and tests. You may want to give a grade for accuracy in keeping the folder.

Activity #3

Do a group KWL Sheet with the students (form included.) Some students will know something about S. E. Hinton or her books and will have information to share. Put this information in the K column (What I Know.) Ask students what they want to find out from reading the book and record this in the W column (What I Want to Find Out.) Keep the sheet and refer back to it after reading the book. Complete the L column (What I Learned) at that time.

Activity #4

Work through the prereading vocabulary worksheet for Chapters 1 & 2 with the students. Tell them they will have a sheet like this to complete before reading each section of the book.

Activity #5

Show students how to preview the study questions for Chapters 1 & 2 of *Rumble Fish*. Encourage students to predict what they think answers might be, to write down their predictions, and to compare these with their answers after reading the chapters.

KWL *Rumble Fish*

Directions: Before reading, think about what you already know about S. E. Hinton and/or *Rumble Fish*. Write the information in the K column. Think about what you would like to find out from reading the book. Write your questions in the W column. After you have read the book, use the L column to write the answers to your questions from the W column, and anything else you remember from the book.

K What I Know	W What I Want To Find Out	L What I Learned

LESSON TWO

Student Objectives
1. To understand the use of flashback in the novel
2. To read Chapters 1 & 2
3. To discuss the main ideas and events in Chapters 1 & 2
4. To become familiar with the Non-Fiction Assignment

Activity #1 Minilesson: Flashback

Flashback is a literary device in which the author inserts a previous event into the current event or scene in the story. It is used to give the reader a better understanding of the character's behavior or motivation in the present. A flashback may take place as a dream or as a memory.
Hinton uses flashback to tell most of the story. The first chapter, when Rusty-James and Steve meet on the beach, is present time. Steve's presence and conversation become the vehicle for Rusty-James to remember the events that comprise most of the book. The scene switches again to the present in the last chapter.

You may want to show a visual illustration of how a flashback is used. A clip from a television show or movie that uses a flashback will be effective. You could also draw a picture of a middle school aged student with a thought balloon over her head. In the thought balloon would be a picture of the student as a baby. Also encourage students to look for clue words such as *thought back to, remembered, reminisced* and *dreamed*. In the last sentence of Chapter 1, Rusty-James says," if he hadn't made me remember everything."

Activity #2

You may want to read Chapter 1 aloud to the students to set the mood for the novel. Invite willing students to read Chapter 2 aloud to the rest of the class.

Activity #3

Divide students into small groups. Give each group one of the study questions to answer. Discuss the answers with the whole class. Write the answers on the board or overhead projector so students can have the correct answers for study purposes. Encourage students to take notes. If they own their copies of *Rumble Fish*, encourage them to use high lighter pens to mark important passages, vocabulary words, and the answers to study guide questions.

Note: It is a good practice in public speaking and leadership skills for individuals students to take charge of leading the discussion of the study questions. Perhaps a different student could go to the front of the class and lead the discussion each day that the study questions are discussed during this unit. Of course, you, the teacher, should guide the discussion when appropriate and be sure to fill in any gaps the students leave. You may also want to give a grade for correct completion of the study guide questions and vocabulary worksheets.

Activity #4

Distribute copies of the Nonfiction Assignment sheet and go over it in detail with the students. Explain to students that they each are to read at least one nonfiction piece at some time during the unit. This could be a book, a magazine article, or information from an encyclopedia or the Internet. Students will fill out a nonfiction assignment sheet after completing the reading to help you (the teacher) evaluate their reading experiences and to help the students think about and evaluate their own reading experiences. Give them the due date for the assignment (Lesson 18.)

Encourage students to read about topics that are related to the theme of the novel. Some suggestions are: Teen-aged gangs; juvenile delinquency, life in low-income neighborhoods, different types of aquarium fish, the effects of close living quarters and poor living conditions on people, and the effects of divorce on children.

NONFICTION ASSIGNMENT SHEET_*Rumble Fish*
(To be completed after reading the required nonfiction article)

Name _____ Date _____ Class _____

Title of Nonfiction Read _____

Written By _____ Publication Date _____

I. Factual Summary: Write a short summary of the piece you read.

II. Vocabulary:
    1. Which vocabulary words were difficult?

    2. What did you do to help yourself understand the words?

III. Interpretation: What was the main point the author wanted you to get from reading his/her work?

IV. Criticism:
    1. Which points of the piece did you agree with or find easy to believe? Why?

    2. With which points of the piece did you disagree or find difficult to believe? Why?

V. Personal Response:
    1. What do you think about this piece?

    2. How does this piece help you better understand the novel *Rumblefish*?

LESSON THREE

Student Objectives
    1. To practice correct intonation and expression in oral reading
    2. To complete the pre-reading vocabulary work for Chapter 3
    3. To preview study questions for Chapters 3
    4. To read Chapter 3 orally for evaluation
    5. To discuss the main ideas and events in Chapter 3

Activity #1

    Give the students about ten minutes to complete the prereading vocabulary worksheet and look over the study guide questions.

Activity #2

    Tell students their oral reading ability will be evaluated. Show them copies of the Oral Reading Evaluation Form and discuss it. Model correct intonation and expression by reading the first few paragraphs of Chapter 3 aloud.

Activity #3

    Call on individual students to read a few paragraphs aloud. Encourage the other students to follow along silently in their books. If you have a student who is unwilling or unable to read in front of the group make arrangements to do his or her evaluation privately at another time.

Activity #4

    Give students about ten minutes to answer the study guide questions. Encourage them to answer as many as they can without looking in the book. Then they can reread to find any answers they didn't know from recall, and to check all of their answers.

Activity #5

    Go over the answers to the study guide questions with students.

ORAL READING EVALUATION *Rumble Fish*

Name_____Class_____Date _____--

SKILL	EXCELLENT	GOOD	AVERAGE	FAIR	POOR
Fluency	5	4	3	2	1
Clarity	5	4	3	2	1
Audibility	5	4	3	2	1
Pronunciation	5	4	3	2	1
_____	5	4	3	2	1
_____	5	4	3	2	1

Total _____ Grade _____

Comments:

LESSON FOUR

Student Objectives
1. To identify the types of conflict in the novel
2. To become familiar with the vocabulary for Chapters 4 & 5
3. To preview the study questions for Chapters 4 & 5
4. To read Chapters 4 & 5
5. To review the main ideas and themes in Chapters 4 & 5
6. To identify foreshadowing in the novel

Activity #1 Minilesson: Conflict
    Tell students that conflict is one of the most important aspects of a work of fiction. The conflict usually is an obstacle to the main character's goal. It usually brings about some type of change in the main character. The types of conflict that are evident in *Rumble Fish* are character vs. character, character vs. himself, and character vs. society.

    You may want to use examples from stories the students have previously read, or examples from literature for younger children to illustrate the various types of conflict. Dorothy in *The Wizard of Oz* has a conflict with nature because the tornado takes her away from her home. The conflict between Cinderella and her wicked step-mother is an example of character vs. character. In *The Little Engine That Could*, the little engine is not sure of its ability to take the train over the mountain, illustrating the character vs. himself conflict. The Greek myth of Atalanta illustrates character vs. society or the environment. Atalanta was expected to marry the man her father chose, but she did not wish to do so.

    Have students begin filling out the Conflict Chart after they have read Chapters 4 & 5. Discuss their findings. Encourage them to look for more examples of conflict as they read. Tell them they will discuss conflict again in Lesson 11.

Activity #2
    Give students about ten minutes to complete the prereading vocabulary worksheet. Students who finish early can draw or cut out magazine pictures to illustrate the vocabulary words.

Activity #3
    Guide the students through the reading of Chapters 4 & 5. Ask the first study guide question. Have students read silently only until they have found the answer. Discuss the answer, then ask question 2. Continue through the chapter this way until all six questions have been answered. Allow time for students to work on their conflict charts.

Activity #4
    The last few paragraphs of Chapter 5 contain an element of foreshadowing regarding Officer Patterson. Have students predict what might happen if he is out to get the boys.

CONFLICT CHART

Directions: Use the chart below to record examples of the different types of conflict you read about in *Rumble Fish*.

Conflict	Example and Pages	Comments
CHARACTER VS. NATURE		
CHARACTER VS. SELF		
CHARACTER VS. SOCIETY		
CHARACTER VS. CHARACTER		

LESSON FIVE

Student Objective
1. To demonstrate understanding of the main ideas and events in Chapters 1-5
2. To write a personal opinion paper

Activity #1
Distribute multiple choice quiz/study questions for Chapters 1-5. Give students about 15 minutes to complete the quiz, then collect the papers.

Activity #2
Write the word *opinion* on the board and ask students what it means. Invite them to give their opinions on topics such as what should be served for lunch in the school cafeteria, if the school should have a dress code, their favorite singer/group. Ask other students to agree or disagree, and state their reasons. Make the point that all people have opinions. A person expressing an opinion should be able to back it up with facts and reasons why he/she has the opinion.

Activity #3
Distribute copies of Writing Assignment #1. Go over the assignment in detail with the students. Tell them they will have the remainder of the class period to begin working on the assignment. Give the due date for the completed assignment. It should be a few days before the writing conferences, which are scheduled for Lesson 9.

Activity #4
Distribute copies of the Writing Evaluation Form (included with this Unit Plan.) Explain to students that during Lesson 9 you will be holding individual writing conferences about this writing assignment. Make sure students are familiar with the criteria on the Writing Evaluation Form.

Follow Up: After you have graded the assignments, have a writing conference with each student. This Unit Plan schedules one in Lesson 9. After the writing conference, allow students to revise their papers using your suggestions to complete the revisions. Grade the revisions on an A-C-E scale: A = all revisions well done; C = some revisions made; E = few or no revisions made. This will speed your grading time and still give some credit for the students' efforts.

WRITING ASSIGNMENT #1 *Rumble Fish*
Writing to Express a Personal Opinion

PROMPT
Rusty-James and the Motorcycle Boy have definite opinions about drugs, gangs, and alcohol. Steve had an opinion about stealing. Rusty-James was angry that Biff was doped up for the fight. The Motorcycle Boy put an end to the gangs. He also told Rusty-James he would break his arm if he ever did drugs, and broke up with Cassandra because she was using heroin. Steve was angry with Rusty-James for stealing the hubcaps. Drugs, alcohol, gangs, and stealing are topics that affect students of your age. What is your opinion about these topics? Your assignment is to choose one and write about it.

PREWRITING
Make a two-column list on a piece of paper. In one column, list drugs, alcohol, gangs, stealing, and any other topics on which you have an opinion. Next to each, briefly jot down your opinion. Then choose the one you want to write about in more depth. Before you begin writing, spend some time thinking about the topic and your opinion. You may want to do some reading so you have evidence to support your opinion. You may also want to talk to others, such as guidance counselors, law-enforcement officials, other adults, or friends.

DRAFTING
Your opening statement should state the topic and give your opinion about it. Give a little bit of background about the topic, and why you chose to write about it. In the next paragraph, state your most important reason. Explain your reason with personal experiences or facts about the topic. Write one paragraph for each reason. In your closing paragraph, state your topic and opinion again.

PEER CONFERENCE/REVISING
When you finish the rough draft, ask another student to look at it. You may want to give the student your brainstorm list so he/she can double check for you and see that you have included all of the information. After reading, he or she should tell you what he/she liked best about your opinion paper, if you stated your opinion clearly and supported it, which parts were difficult to understand or needed more information, and ways in which your work could be improved. Reread your opinion paper considering your critic's comments and make the corrections you think are necessary.

PROOFREADING/EDITING
Do a final proofreading of your opinion paper, double-checking your grammar, spelling, organization, and the clarity of your ideas.

WRITING EVALUATION FORM *Rumble Fish*

Name _____ Date _____ Class _____

<u>Writing Assignment # 1 Writing to Express a Personal Opinion</u>

Circle One For Each Item:

| <u>Composition</u> | excellent | good | fair | poor |

<u>Composition</u>   excellent   good   fair   poor

<u>Style</u>   excellent   good   fair   poor

<u>Grammar</u>   excellent   good   fair   poor (errors noted)

<u>Spelling</u>   excellent   good   fair   poor (errors noted)

<u>Punctuation</u>   excellent   good   fair   poor (errors noted)

<u>Legibility</u>   excellent   good   fair   poor (errors noted)

<u>Strengths:</u>

<u>Weaknesses:</u>

<u>Comments/Suggestions:</u>

LESSON SIX

Student Objectives
    1. To understand character development by discussing Rusty-James
    2. To become familiar with the vocabulary for Chapters 6 & 7
    3. To preview the study questions for Chapters 6 & 7

Activity #1: Minilesson: Character Development

    Explain that an author creates a character, in this case Rusty-James, by giving him traits such as physical attributes, thoughts, and feelings. The author develops these traits by telling what the character says, does, and thinks. Writers usually base their characters at least in part on a real person or persons, and then elaborate. A good writer will make the characters believable for the readers.

    Have students look for Rusty-James's character traits in the chapters they have already read. Help them begin filling in the Character Trait Chart (included.) Tell them they should continue to be aware of Rusty-James's character as they read, and that they will continue the discussion and complete more of the chart during Lesson 11.

Activity #2

    Use the rest of the period for independent work. Have students do the prereading vocabulary worksheet and study guide questions for Chapters 6 & 7. If they have time, they can begin reading silently. Tell students they should have the reading and study questions for Chapters 6 & 7 completed before the next class period.

LESSON SEVEN

Student Objectives
    1. To discuss the main ideas and events in Chapters 6 & 7
    2. To complete the prereading vocabulary work for Chapters 8 & 9
    3. To preview the study questions for Chapters 8 & 9
    4. To read Chapters 8 & 9 aloud
    5. To add to the conflict chart

Activity #1

    Divide the class into teams of about 5 students each. Ask the study guide questions one at a time and have one member of the team write down the group's answer. After all questions have been asked, discuss the answers. Have one person in each group act as the checker. Give each team one point for each correct answer. Tally the points. The team with the highest number of points could receive a treat, such as a food treat, a few minutes of free time. Each team could receive extra credit points based on the number of correct responses.

Activity #2

    Give students about fifteen minutes to complete the prereading vocabulary work and study guide questions.

Activity #3

    Ask for volunteers to take the parts of a narrator and the characters in Chapters 8 & 9. Have them read the chapters aloud as an old-fashioned radio play as the rest of the students listen.

Activity #4

    Give students a few minutes to add information to the conflict and character sketch charts.

LESSON EIGHT

Student Objectives
1. To discuss the main ideas and events in Chapters 8 & 9
2. To complete Writing Assignment #2

Activity #1
Divide the class into small groups. Have each group make a drawing to illustrate the answer to one of the study guide questions. Then have one member of each group describe the drawing and discuss the answer.

Activity #2
Distribute copies of Writing Assignment #2. Give students the rest of the period to complete the assignment. If students need extra time, set a due date for the assignment.

LESSON NINE

Student Objectives
1. To participate in a writing conference with the teacher
2. To become familiar with the vocabulary for Chapters 10-12
3. To preview the study guide questions for Chapters 10-12
4. To read Chapters 10-12
5. To revise Writing Assignment #1 based on the teacher's suggestions

Activity #1
Hold individual reading conferences in a quiet corner of the room.

Activity #2
Have students revise the assignments during class time or as a home assignment.

Activity #3
Students may use the rest of the class time while you are conferencing for doing the prereading vocabulary worksheet, reading the chapters, and preparing the answers to the study guide questions.

WRITING ASSIGNMENT #2 *Rumble Fish*
Writing to Inform

PROMPT

You are enjoying the book *Rumblefish*, and want to let others know about it. Your assignment is to write a cinquain poem to highlight the parts of the book you like the most.

PREWRITING

Make a list of the characters and events you like in the novel. Then choose the ones you want to write about.

DRAFTING

A cinquain poem has five lines and follows a formula. Choose the formula you want to use. You may want to try one of each and decide which you like the best. Then make a draft of your poem.

Line 1--- 2 syllables
Line 2--- 4 syllables
Line 3--- 6 syllables
Line 4--- 8 syllables
Line 5--- 2 syllables

Another variation has the following format:
Line 1--- noun
Line 2--- two adjectives
Line 3--- three gerunds (ing verbs)
Line 4--- a five to seven word phrase or sentence
Line 5--- a synonym for line one

PEER CONFERENCING/REVISING

When you finish the rough draft, ask another student to look at it. After reading, he or she should tell you what he/she liked best about your cinquain which parts were difficult to understand or needed more information, and ways in which your work could be improved. Reread your cinquain poem considering your critic's comments and make the corrections you think are necessary.

PROOFREADING/EDITING

Do a final proofreading of your cinquain poem, double-checking your grammar, spelling, organization, and the clarity of your ideas.

LESSON TEN

Student Objectives
1. To discuss the main ideas and details in Chapters 10-12
2. To complete a story map
3. To complete all previous assignments

Activity #1

Give each student four 1"x2" strips of colored paper or index cards--one blue, one yellow, one green, one pink. Have them put a large letter A on the blue paper, B on the yellow, C on the green, and D on the pink. Distribute copies of the Multiple Choice/Quiz questions for Chapters 10-12. Ask students to read the first question and hold up the colored paper for the correct answer. Then have them mark the correct answer on their worksheets.

Activity #2 Minilesson: Story Elements, Story Map

Review the elements of a story. Then help students complete the story map. You may want to have students draw a picture on the back of the paper to illustrate the items on the story map.
Setting: Where and when the story takes place; time and place.
Characters: The people in the story. Animals can also be considered characters. Major characters are those who are most developed and have the largest role in the story. Minor characters are less developed and have smaller roles in the story.
Plot: What happens in the story. On the story map, Plot is divided into problem and solution, with a separate space for events.
Point of View: This is the focus from which the author writes. In first person the story is told through the eyes of a character, usually the main character, who uses the first person pronoun "I." The reader lives the story as the narrator tells it. In third person omniscient viewpoint, the author knows everything and tells the reader about the actions and thought processes of all of the characters. In the third person limited omniscient viewpoint, the author tells the story in the third person and focuses on the feelings, experiences, and thoughts of one main character. In an objective viewpoint, the author only reveals what can be seen and heard. This viewpoint is similar to that in watching a movie.
Theme: The theme is the meaning of the story. An explicit theme is openly stated in the story. An implicit theme may be understood from analyzing the thoughts, actions, and speech of the characters as they develop and try to overcome their problems or solve conflicts.

Activity #3

Use the rest of the class period to have students go through their notes and worksheets and check to see that all work has been completed.

Activity #4

If students have completed all assignments and there is extra class time, choose one of the Unit Review activities in Lesson 15 and do it now.

STORY MAP *Rumble Fish*

CHARACTERS	SETTING
Main:	Time:
Minor:	Place:

THEME	POINT OF VIEW

PLOT

PROBLEM	EVENTS	SOLUTION

LESSON ELEVEN

Student Objective

To discuss *Rumble Fish* at the interpretive and critical levels

Activity #1

Choose the questions from the Extra Writing Assignments/Discussion Questions which seem most appropriate for your students. A class discussion of these questions is most effective if students have been given the opportunity to formulate answers to the questions prior to the discussion. To this end, you may either have all the students formulate answers to all the questions, divide the class into groups and assign one or more questions to each group, or you could assign one question to each student in your class. The option you choose will make a difference in the amount of class time needed for this activity.

Activity #2

After students have had ample time to formulate answers to the questions, begin your class discussion of the questions and the ideas presented by the questions. Be sure students take notes during the discussion so they have information to study for the unit test.

Activity #3

You may want to complete or review the conflict chart at this time.

LESSON TWELVE

Student Objective

To practice writing to persuade

Activity #1

Distribute copies of Writing Assignment #3 and read over it with students.

Activity #2

Give students the rest of the period to complete the assignment.

EXTRA WRITING ASSIGNMENT/DISCUSSION QUESTIONS
Rumble Fish

1. Summarize the story in ten sentences or less.

2. What are the main conflicts in the story? Are they resolved? If so, how? If not, why not?

3. Discuss the main themes in the novel.

4. Write a character sketch of one of the following: Steve Hays, Rusty-James, the Motorcycle Boy, the boys' father.

5. What is the setting of the story? How important is this to the plot?

6. Rusty-James is upset that Biff has a knife. What do you think of his reason for being upset? What does this show about his personality? Chapter 3

7. Why was Steve crying at the end of Chapter 4?

8. Why did Rusty-James say the pool hall wasn't a cool place to be without the Motorcycle Boy? Chapter 8,

9. Why did the black man tell Rusty-James he would never look like the Motorcycle Boy? Chapter 8

10. Why was the Motorcycle Boy surprised at his own reaction when he found out Rusty-James was alive? Chapter 8

11. Rusty-James said the Motorcycle Boy was alone, living in a glass bubble and watching the world from it. What do you think he meant? Chapter 8

Extra Discussion Questions *Rumble Fish*

Interpretive

12. Rusty-James gives physical descriptions of himself and the Motorcycle Boy, then says people never think they are brothers. Why do you think this is so? Chapter 8

13. The Motorcycle Boy said the only vice Rusty-James had was loyalty. Do you agree or disagree? How can loyalty be a vice?

14. What caused the funny feeling Rusty-James described in Chapter 9?

15. What do you think Steve was realizing about Rusty-James at the end of Chapter 9?

16. Why did the pet store give Rusty-James the creeps? Chapter 10

17. How do you think Rusty-James felt at the end of Chapter 10?

18. Why do you think the Motorcycle Boy broke into the pet store? Why did he turn on the lights?

19. In Chapter 12, Steve tells Rusty-James that if he went back to the old neighborhood, it could give people heart attacks. Why?

20. Why do you think Rusty-James was having trouble with his memory?

21. Does Rusty-James really understand the Motorcycle Boy? Give examples from the story to support your answer.

Critical

22. From which point of view is the story written? How does this affect your understanding and enjoyment of the story?

23. Is the story believable? Why or why not?

24. Steve and Rusty-James are very different personalities. They seem unlikely as best friends. Why do you think Hinton included Steve's character, and made him the way he was?

25. What was the overall mood of the story? Give examples to support your answer.

26. Was the use of flashback effective?

27. How did Hinton's use of slang affect your understanding and enjoyment of the story?

Extra Discussion Questions *Rumble Fish*

28. In Chapter 3, the Motorcycle Boy says he got expelled because he had perfect semester tests. Discuss the irony of this situation.

29. What purpose did the character of Cassandra serve in the story? Was the reference to the Greek Cassandra in Chapter 5 significant? Why or why not?

30. Was the Motorcycle Boy's death necessary to the story? How would the outcome have changed if he had lived?

31. Why do you think S. E. Hinton made the Motorcycle Boy color blind? What is she saying about him?

32. The author never gave the Motorcycle Boy a name. In the novel, the others in the neighborhood gave him his nickname. Why do you think the author wrote his character this way? How effective is it in portraying his personality?

Personal Opinion

33. Did you enjoy reading Rumble Fish? Why or why not?

34. Did you like the ending? Explain your reason.

35. Is *Rumble Fish* a good title for the book? Why or why not? If not, what title would you suggest?

36. Will you read more of S. E. Hinton's books? Why or why not?

37. Did Rusty-James's experiences change the way you look at yourself? How?

38. Would you recommend this book to another student? Why or why not?

QUOTATIONS *Rumble Fish*

1. I can't remember much about it. Like I said, my memory's screwed up. (Chapter 1)

2. "You know who you look just like?"
"Yeah," I said, and remembered everything. (Chapter 1)

3. "He says he's gonna kill you." (Chapter 2)

4. "Lookit, me an' Biff'll settle this thing ourselves. You guys'll just be an audience, huh? Ain't nothin' wrong with an audience." (Chapter 2)

5. "The Motorcycle Boy ain't back," I said. "I don't know when he's comin' back, if he's comin' back. So if you wanna wait around the rest of your life to see what he says, okay. But I'm gonna stomp Biff Wilcox's guts tonight, and I think I oughta have some friends there." (Chapter 2)

6. "You have to face the fact that the Motorcycle Boy may be gone for good."
"I don't have to face nothin'," I said tiredly. (Chapter 2)

7. "You said you were going to quit fighting all the time."
"Since when?"
"Since you beat up Skip Handley. You promised me you wouldn't be fighting all the time."
"Oh, yeah. Well, this ain't all the time. This is just once." (Chapter 3)

8. I love fights. I love how I feel before a fight, kind of high, like I can do anything. (Chapter 3)

9. "Man, this is just like the old days, isn't it?. . . A gang really meant somethin' back then." (Chapter 3)

10. "Hey, what's this? I thought we signed a treaty." (Chapter 3)

11. "I think," he said thoughtfully, "that the show is over." (Chapter 3)

12. "Kid," he said to me, "I never got past the river." (Chapter 3)

13. "Okay, let's get it straight what we're fighting for."
"We're fighting to own this street."
"Bull, We're fighting for fun." (Chapter 3)

Quotations *Rumble Fish*

14. "I handed in perfect semester tests." (Chapter 3)

15. Even if he hadn't been my brother he would have been the coolest person in the whole world. And I was going to be just like him. (Chapter 3)

16. "Hey, man! You been to the nurse?" (Chapter 4)

17. "You know I don't steal things".
    "You know I *do*." I answered. (Chapter 4)

18. "He don't like you," I went on. "Any more than he liked any of the rest of them."
    "He don't like me now, period. See?" (Chapter 5)

19. "Russell-James," he said suddenly. "Are you ill?"
    "Got cut up in a knife fight," I told him."
    "Really?" He came over to take a look. "What strange lives you two lead."
    "I ain't so strange," I said.
    He gave me a ten dollar bill. (Chapter 5)

20. "Did you have a nice trip?"
    "Yeah. Went to California."
    "How was California?"
    "It was one laugh after another. Even better than here, as amusing as this place is." (Ch. 5)

21. "You are exactly like your mother." (Chapter 5)

22. "Don't you think it's time you gave some serious thought to your life?" (Chapter 6)

23. "Just get lost. I don't want to ever see your face again." (Chapter 6)

24. "It's a bit of a burden to be Robin Hood, Jesse James and the Pied Piper. I'd just as soon stay a neighborhood novelty, if it's all the same to you. It's not that I couldn't handle a larger scale, I just plain don't want to." (Chapter 6)

25. "That was pretty good," said the Motorcycle Boy. "Did you ever think of trying out for a chameleon?"
    "I don't know them," I said, kind of proud of myself. "Where's their turf?"

Quotations *Rumble Fish*

26. "Sometimes, it seems to me like I can remember colors, 'way back when I was a little kid. That was a long time ago. I stopped bein' a little kid when I was five."
"Yeah? I wonder when I'm gonna stop bein' a little kid."
"Never." (Chapter 7)

27. "California is like a beautiful wild kid on heroin, high as a kite and thinking she's on top of the world, not knowing she's dying, not believing it even if you show her the marks."
(Chapter 7)

28. "My, my, my. Ain't he fine?"
"Yeah. And I'm gonna look just like him."
"No you ain't, baby. That cat is a prince, man. He is royalty in exile. You ain't *never* gonna look like that." (Chapter 8)

29. "He ain't dead." (Chapter 8)

30. "What a funny situation. I wonder what I'm doing here, holding my half-dead brother, surrounded by bricks and cement and rats. Although I suppose it's a s good a place to be as any. There weren't so many walls in California, but if you're used to walls all that air can give you the creeps."
(Chapter 8)

31. "Will you shut up about that! The rumbles! The gang! That garbage! It wasn't anything. It wasn't anything like you think it was. It was just a bunch of punks killing each other!"
(Chapter 8)

32. "Apparently it is essential to some people to belong--anywhere." (Chapter 8)

33. "I've tried to help you. But I've got to think about myself some. You're just like a ball in a pinball machine. Getting slammed back and forth; and you never think about anything, about where you're going or how to get there. I got to think for myself, I can't keep on thinking for you, too." (Chapter 9)

34. "If you're around him very long you won't believe in anything."
"I been around him all my life. And I believe in everything."
"You would."
"Bye."
Rusty-James, I'm sorry."
"Sure." (Chapter 9)

Quotations *Rumble Fish*

35. "She said, 'Tell Rusty-James that life goes on, if you let it.' Do you know what she meant? (Chapter 10)

36. "Rumble fish. They'd kill each other if they could." (Chapter 10)

37. "I think that I'm gonna look just like him when I get older. Whadd'ya think?"
"You better pray to God not. You poor child. You poor baby." (Chapter 11)

38. I was so scared I dropped my head down on the counter and cried for the first time I could remember. Crying hurts like hell. (Chapter 11)

39. "Can you hear me?" (Chapter 11)

40. "I made up my mind I'd get out of that place and I did. I learned that. I learned that if you want to get somewhere, you just make up your mind and work like hell till you get there. If you want to go somewhere in life you just have to work till you make it." (Chapter 12)

41. ". . . right about that. I never thought you would, but you do. You don't sound like him, though. Your voice is completely different. It's a good thing you never went back. You'd probably give half the people in the neighborhood a heart attack." (Chapter 12)

WRITING ASSIGNMENT #3 *Rumble Fish*
Writing to Persuade

PROMPT
In Chapter 9, Steve says to Rusty James, "I've tried to help you, but I've got to think about myself some." Earlier, Steve was upset when Rusty-James stole the hubcaps. In Chapter 12, Steve told Rusty-James he used to worry about the amount he drank. These scenes show Steve's concern for his friend's welfare. Pretend you are one of Rusty-James's friends. What would you say to him to try and convince him to change his ways and adopt a healthier life style?

PREWRITING
Make a list of the reasons you think Rusty-James should change. Think of statements to support each of your reasons, and list them under each reason. Then number the reasons in order from most to least important.

DRAFTING
Make an introductory statement in which you state what you want and why.
Use one paragraph for each of your reasons. Use the supporting statements for each reason.
Summarize your talk by restating what you want.

PEER CONFERENCING/REVISING
When you finish the rough draft, ask another student to look at it. You may want to give the student your checklist so he/she can double check for you and see that you have included all of the information. After reading, he or she should tell you what he/she liked best about your persuasive talk, which parts were difficult to understand or needed more information, and ways in which your work could be improved. Reread your persuasive talk considering your critic's comments and make the corrections you think are necessary.

PROOFREADING/EDITING
Do a final proofreading of your persuasive talk, double-checking your grammar, spelling, organization, and the clarity of your ideas.

FINAL DRAFT
Follow your teacher's guidelines for completing the final draft of your persuasive talk.

LESSON THIRTEEN

Student Objectives
1. To extend the story by means of a project
2. To work cooperatively in a group

Activity

Allow students to choose one of the following projects. Give them the class period to complete it. If students need more time, you can assign the project as homework or add another day onto the unit plan.

PROJECT IDEAS

1. Draw a book jacket that summarizes the story.

2. Write a critique of the book.

3. Make a timeline showing the important events from the story.

4. Make a diorama showing one of the scenes from the book.

5. Make clay models of the characters in the book.

6. Make puppets and write a puppet show to illustrate one scene from the story.

7. Write a radio or television commercial to advertise the book.

8. Design a poster to advertise the book.

9. Write a different ending to the story.

10. Make a comic book version of the story to share with younger readers.

11. Make a mobile showing the main character, secondary characters and setting.

12. Make a collage based on scenes from the book.

13. Choose a scene from the book and develop a skit. Perform it for the class.

14. Prepare to make a movie version of the novel. Choose actors to play the parts of the characters. Choose a location for shooting the movie.

LESSON FOURTEEN

Student Objective
   To review all of the vocabulary work done in this unit

VOCABULARY REVIEW ACTIVITIES

1. Divide your class into two teams and have an old-fashioned spelling or definition bee.

2. Give individuals or groups of students a *Rumble Fish* Vocabulary Word Search Puzzle. The person (group) to find all of the vocabulary words in the puzzle first wins.

3. Give students a *Rumble Fish* Vocabulary Word Search Puzzle without the word list. The person or group to find the most vocabulary words in the puzzle wins.

4. Put a *Rumble Fish* Vocabulary Crossword Puzzle onto a transparency on the overhead projector and do the puzzle together as a class.

5. Give students a *Rumble Fish* Vocabulary Matching Worksheet to do.

6. Use words from the word jumble page and have students spell them correctly.

7. Have students write a story in which they correctly use as many vocabulary words as possible. Have students read their compositions orally. Post the most original compositions on your bulletin board.

8. Have students work in teams and play charades with the vocabulary words.

9. Select a word of the day and encourage students to use it correctly in their writing and speaking vocabulary.

10. Have a contest to see which students can find the most vocabulary words used in other sources. You may want to have a bulletin board available so the students can write down their word, the sentence it was used in, and the source.

11. Assign a word to each student, or let them choose a word. Have them look up the origin of the word, the part of speech, definition, a synonym, and an antonym. Then have them write a sentence using the word. Have students present their information orally to the class, or have them design a word map on paper and display the papers.

LESSON FIFTEEN

Objective
   To review the main ideas presented in *Rumble Fish*

Activity #1
   Choose one of the review games/activities included in the packet and spend your class period as outlined there.

Activity #2
   Remind students of the date for the Unit Test. Stress the review of the Study Guides and their class notes as a last minute, brush-up review for homework.

REVIEW GAMES / ACTIVITIES

1. Ask the class to make up a unit test for *Rumble Fish*. The test should have 4 sections: multiple choice, true/false, short answer and essay. Students may use 1/2 period to make the test, including a separate answer sheet, and then swap papers and use the other 1/2 class period to take a test a classmate has devised. (open book)

2. Take 1/2 period for students to make up true and false questions (including the answers). Collect the papers and divide the class into two teams. Draw a big tic-tac-toe board on the chalk board. Make one team X and one team O. Ask questions to each side, giving each student one turn. If the question is answered correctly, that student's team's letter (X or O) is placed in the box. If the answer is incorrect, no mark is placed in the box. The object is to get three marks in a row like tic-tac-toe. You may want to keep track of the number of games won for each team.

3. Take 1/2 period for students to make up questions (true/false and short answer). Collect the questions. Divide the class into two teams. You'll alternate asking questions to individual members of teams A & B (like in a spelling bee). The question keeps going from A to B until it is correctly answered, then a new question is asked. A correct answer does not allow the team to get another question. Correct answers are +2 points; incorrect answers are -1 point.

4. Allow students time to quiz each other (in pairs) from their study guides and class notes.

5. Give students a *Rumble Fish* crossword puzzle to complete.

REVIEW GAMES / ACTIVITIES

6. Divide your class into two teams. Use the *Rumble Fish* crossword words with their letters jumbled as a word list. Student 1 from Team A faces off against Student 1 from Team B. You write the first jumbled word on the board. The first student (1A or 1B) to unscramble the word wins the chance for his/her team to score points. If 1A wins the jumble, go to student 2A and give him/her a clue. He/she must give you the correct word which matches that clue. If he/she does, Team A scores a point, and you give student 3A a clue for which you expect another correct response. Continue giving Team A clues until some team member makes an incorrect response. An incorrect response sends the game back to the jumbled-word face off, this time with students 2A and 2B. Instead of repeating giving clues to the first few students of each team, continue with the student after the one who gave the last incorrect response on the team.

7. Take on the persona of "The Answer Person." Allow students to ask any question about the book. Answer the questions, or tell students where to look in the book to find the answer.

8. Students may enjoy playing charades with events from the story. Select a student to start. Give him/her a card with a scene or event from the story. Allow the players to use their books to find the scene being described. The first person to guess each charade performs the next one.

9. Play a categories-type quiz game. (A master is included in this Unit Plan). Make an overhead transparency of the categories form. Divide the class into teams of three or four players each. Have each team choose a recorder and a banker. Choose a team to go first. That team will choose a category and point amount. Ask the question to the entire class.(Use the Study Guide Quiz and Vocabulary questions.) Give the teams one minute to discuss the answer and write it down. Walk around the room and check the answers. Each team that answers correctly receives the points. (Incorrect answers are not penalized; they just don't receive any points). Cross out that square on the playing board. Play continues until all squares have been used. The winning team is the one with the most points. You can assign bonus points to any square or squares you choose.

10. Have individual students draw scenes from the book. Display the scenes and have the rest of the class look in their books to find the chapter or section that is being depicted. The first student to find the correct scene then displays his or her picture. When the game is over, collect the pictures and put them in a binder for students to look at during their free time.

NOTE: If students do not need the extra review, omit this lesson and go on to the test.

QUIZ GAME
Rumble Fish

Chapters 1-3	Chapters 4-5	Chapters 6-7	Chapters 8-9	Chapters 10-12
100	100	100	100	100
200	200	200	200	200
300	300	300	300	300
400	400	400	400	400
500	500	500	500	500

LESSON SIXTEEN

Objective
   To test the students' understanding of the main ideas and themes in *Rumblefish*

Activity #1
   Distribute the *Rumble Fish* Unit Tests. Go over the instructions in detail and allow the students the entire class period to complete the exam.

Activity #2
   Collect all test papers and assigned books prior to the end of the class period.

NOTES ABOUT THE UNIT TESTS IN THIS UNIT:
There are 5 different unit tests which follow.

There are two short answer tests which are based primarily on facts from the novel. The answer key for short answer unit test 1 follows the student test. The answer key for short answer test 2 follows the student short answer unit test 2.

There is one advanced short answer unit test. It is based on the extra discussion questions. Use the matching key for short answer unit test 2 to check the matching section of the advanced short answer unit test. There is no key for the short answer questions. The answers will be based on the discussions you have had during class.

There are two multiple choice unit tests. Following the two unit tests, you will find an answer sheet on which students should mark their answers. The same answer sheet should be used for both tests; however, students' answers will be different for each test. Following the students' answer sheet for the multiple choice tests you will find your answer keys.

The short answer tests have a vocabulary section. You should choose 10 of the vocabulary words from this unit, read them orally and have the students write them down. Then, either have students write a definition or use the words in sentences. The second part of the vocabulary test is matching.

LESSON SEVENTEEN

Objectives
>   1. To widen the breadth of students' knowledge about the topics discussed or touched upon in *Rumble Fish*
>   2. To check students' non-fiction assignments

Activity

Ask each student to give a brief oral report about the nonfiction work he/she read for the nonfiction assignment. Your criteria for evaluating this report will vary depending on the level of your students. You may wish for students to give a complete report without using notes of any kind, or you may want students to read directly from a written report, or you may want to do something in between these two extremes. Just make students aware of your criteria in ample time for them to prepare their reports.

Start with one student's report. After that, ask if anyone else in the class has read on a topic related to the first student's report. If no one has, choose another student at random. After each report, be sure to ask if anyone has a report related to the one just completed. That will help keep a continuity during the discussion of the reports.

LESSON EIGHTEEN

Objectives
>   1. To watch a movie version of the novel *Rumble Fish*
>   2. To compare and contrast the movie with the novel
>   3. To listen to the audio cassette rendition of the novel

Activity #1

The movie version of *Rumble Fish* is available in many video stores, and through educational film distributors. Show the movie in class. Note: Since the movie version differs somewhat from the book, it is recommended to show it after giving the test.

Activity #2

Discuss the ways in which the movie and the novel were similar and different. Discuss the reasons for the differences. You may want the students to write a short comparison/contrast paper after this discussion, or record their observations on a Venn Diagram chart.

Activity #3

Listen to the audio cassette version of the novel.

Note: This activity may take two class periods, depending on the length of your class.

UNIT TESTS

SHORT ANSWER UNIT TEST 1 *Rumble Fish*

I. Matching/ Identify

_____ 1. Cleveland   A. He didn't belong anywhere.
_____ 2. loyalty   B. Steve's ___ beat him for staying out late.
_____ 3. California   C. It didn't scare Rusty-James.
_____ 4. father   D. It was Rusty-James's only vice.
_____ 5. Steve Hays   E. The Motorcycle Boy's ___ scared Rusty-James.
_____ 6. the Motorcycle Boy F. It was Biff's territory.
_____ 7. mother   G. He spent five years in a reformatory.
_____ 8. smile   H. He recognized his old friend on the beach.
_____ 9. Rusty-James   I. The Motorcycle Boy went on a trip there.
_____ 10. pain   J. Rusty-James's ___ left the family when he was two.

II. Short Answer

1. Rusty-James has two problems in Chapter 2. What are they, and how are they solved?

2. How did Rusty-James feel about his father? How did he feel about the Motorcycle Boy?

Short Answer Unit Test 1 *Rumble Fish*

3. In Chapters 6 and 7, Rusty-James had a problem at school and one with his girlfriend. Describe the problems and the outcomes.

4. Describe the scene at Steve's house after Rusty-James left the clinic. (Chapters 8 & 9)

5. Discuss the meaning of the following quotation from Chapter 11: "I was so scared I dropped my head down on the counter and cried for the first time I could remember. Crying hurts like hell."

Short Answer Unit Test 1 *Rumble Fish*

III. Fill in the Blanks
Write the word or words to correctly complete each sentence about the story.

1. Most of the story is told in _____.

2. During the fight with Biff, Rusty-James was _____.

3. Rusty-James was fourteen, and wanted to be just like _____, who was seventeen.

4. Rusty-James did not have a very good home life. His father _____ most of the time.

5. For a while, Rusty-James was the top tough guy, until _____ stole his girlfriend and also told him the other guys would not follow him into a fight because he would get them all killed.

7. On a trip to the city one night, Rusty-James was almost _____.

8. The Motorcycle Boy told Rusty-James that he had seen _____.

9. One night, the Motorcycle Boy broke into the _____

10. As he was running toward the river, he was _____. Rusty-James tried hard to forget about that night.

Short Answer Unit Test 1 *Rumble Fish*

IV. <u>Essay</u>

What are the main conflicts in the story? Are they resolved? If so, how? If not, why not?

Short Answer Unit Test 1 *Rumble Fish*

V. Vocabulary Part 1

Listen to the vocabulary words and spell them. After you have spelled all the words, go back and write down the definitions.

WORD **DEFINITION**

1. _____   _____
2. _____   _____
3. _____   _____
4. _____   _____
5. _____   _____
6. _____   _____
7. _____   _____
8. _____   _____
9. _____   _____
10. _____   _____

Vocabulary Part 2

Directions: Place the letter of the matching definition on the blank line.

_____ 1. acute   A. difficult
_____ 2. complicated   B. offensive; annoying
_____ 3. distorted   C. permit; endure
_____ 4. innate   D. inherited; inborn
_____ 5. obnoxious   E. intense
_____ 6. perception   F. empty
_____ 7. simulated   G. imitation
_____ 8. tension   H. insight
_____ 9. tolerate   I. deformed; twisted out of shape
_____ 10. vacant   J. anxiety; unease

ANSWER KEY SHORT ANSWER UNIT TEST 1 *Rumble Fish*

F	1.	Cleveland	A.	He didn't belong anywhere.
D	2.	loyalty	B.	Steve's __ beat him for staying out late.
I	3.	California	C.	It didn't scare Rusty-James.
B	4.	father	D.	It was Rusty-James's only vice.
H	5.	Steve Hays	E.	The Motorcycle Boy's __ scared Rusty-James.
A	6.	the Motorcycle Boy	F.	It was Biff's territory.
J	7.	mother	G.	He spent five years in a reformatory.
E	8.	smile	H.	He recognized his old friend on the beach.
G	9.	Rusty-James	I.	The Motorcycle Boy went on a trip there.
C	10.	pain	J.	Rusty-James's __ left the family when he was two.

II. Short Answer

1. Rusty-James had two problems in Chapter 2. What were they, and how were they solved?
    Biff Wilcox wanted to fight him, and the Motorcycle Boy had not returned from his trip. Rusty-James was not sure if he would come back at all. Rusty-James and a few of his friends went to the field to meet Biff. They fought, and Biff knifed him. The Motorcycle Boy returned and stopped the fight.

2. How did Rusty-James feel about his father? How did he feel about the Motorcycle Boy?
    He wasn't sure exactly how he felt about his father. They got along okay, but didn't talk much. Rusty-James found it hard to respect his father, because he didn't do any work. He thought his father liked him more than he liked the Motorcycle Boy. He thought the wanted to be just like the Motorcycle Boy.

3. In Chapters 6 and 7, Rusty-James had a problem at school and one with his girlfriend. Describe the problems and the outcomes.

    He was expelled. The guidance counselor told him he would be transferred to Cleveland High School. Rusty-James didn't want to go there, because Biff and his friends ran the school. The counselor said the alternative was the Youth Detention Center. Rusty-James decided to take his chances and stay out of school altogether until the Detention Center caught up with him. He thought he had a few weeks to figure out what to do.

Patty got off the bus and ignored him. Then she said she was breaking up with him because he had been with another girl at the lake. Rusty-James didn't understand what his being with a girl at the lake had to do with him and Patty. He wondered if he was going to cry, but he felt better in a little while.

4. Describe the scene at Steve's house after Rusty-James left the clinic. (Chapters 8 & 9.)
Rusty-James went to Steve's house after the left the clinic. He had never been there before. Steve's father had beaten him up for getting home so late. Steve defended his father to Rusty-James. He asked Rusty-James to say he got beat up during their confrontation with the two boys in the city.

5. Discuss the meaning of the following quotation from Chapter 11: "I was so scared I dropped my head down on the counter and cried for the first time I could remember. Crying hurts like hell."
Rusty-James was in the pet store with the Motorcycle Boy. The Motorcycle Boy had just released all of the animals. Rusty-James was trying to get him to stop, but the Motorcycle Boy was not paying attention to him.

III. Fill in the Blanks
Write the word or words to correctly complete each sentence about the story.

1. Most of the story is told in **flashback**.
2. During the fight with Biff, Rusty-James was **knifed in the side.**
3. Rusty-James was fourteen, and wanted to be just like **The Motorcycle Boy,** who was seventeen.
4. Rusty-James did not have a very good home life. His father **drank/went to bars** most of the time.
5. For a while, Rusty-James was the top tough guy, until **Smokey** stole his girlfriend and also told him the other guys would not follow him into a fight because he would get them all killed.
7. On a trip to the city one night, Rusty-James was almost **killed.**
8. The Motorcycle Boy told Rusty-James that he had seen **their mother in California.**
9. One night, the Motorcycle Boy broke into the **pet store.**
10. As he was running toward the river, The Motorcycle Boy was **shot and killed** by Officer Patterson. Rusty-James tried hard to forget about that night.

IV. Vocabulary Part 1

Choose any ten words from the pre-reading vocabulary words to dictate for this section of the test

Vocabulary Part 2

E	1.	acute	A.	difficult
A	2.	complicated	B.	offensive; annoying
I	3.	distorted	C.	permit; endure
D	4.	innate	D.	inherited; inborn
B	5.	obnoxious	E.	intense
H	6.	perception	F.	empty
G	7.	simulated	G.	imitation
J	8.	tension	H.	insight
C	9.	tolerate	I.	deformed; twisted out of shape
F	10.	vacant	J.	anxiety; unease

SHORT ANSWER UNIT TEST 2 *Rumble Fish*

I. Matching/ Identify

____ 1. Cassandra   A. owned the pet store
____ 2. Patty   B. didn't like it when Rusty-James fought.
____ 3. Jeannie   C. was expelled because of perfect semester tests.
____ 4. Mr. Harrigan   D. liked the Motorcycle Boy.
____ 5. Mr. Donnely   E. shot the Motorcycle Boy.
____ 6. Coach Ryan   F. liked Steve but not Rusty-James.
____ 7. Patterson   G. got out of the old neighborhood and went to college.
____ 8. Rusty-James   H. wanted Rusty-James to beat up a student.
____ 9. the Motorcycle Boy   I. was the school guidance counselor.
____ 10. Steve   J. was suspended because of bad behavior.

II. Short Answer

1. Describe the fight with Biff. Include the way it ended.

2. How did Rusty-James feel about his father? How did he feel about the Motorcycle Boy?

Short Answer Unit Test 2 *Rumble Fish*

3. How did Rusty-James describe the feeling when the black guy hit him? How was Rusty-James saved?

4. Describe the scene between Smokey and Rusty-James at Benny's.

5. Discuss the significance of the following quotation: "I can't remember much about it. Like I said, my memory's screwed up."

Short Answer Unit Test 2 *Rumble Fish*

III. Fill in the Blank

Write the word or words to correctly complete each sentence about the story.

1. When the story opened, Rusty-James was sitting on a beach. He had recently been released after spending five years in a _____.

2. Rusty-James did not have a very settled life. He and his older brother lived with their _____, who drank most of the time.

3. Rusty and Biff _____.

4. There weren't any gangs anymore. The Motorcycle Boy said it was because _____ had ruined them. Rusty-James missed them, and wanted them back.

5. Rusty-James continued to get into trouble. He was expelled from school, and his girlfriend, Patty _____.

6. Smokey told Rusty-James he was not the _____. The other boys would not follow him into a fight, because they thought he would get them killed.

7. Near the end of the story, Rusty-James followed his brother as he _____.

8. The Motorcycle Boy took the _____ to the river.

9. Rusty-James was behind his brother and heard the shot. He arrived to find _____.

10. The story went back to the present. His old friend has asked him to meet for dinner. Rusty-James knew that he _____ see his friend for dinner.

Short Answer Unit Test 2 *Rumble Fish*

IV. <u>Essay</u>

Rusty-James said the Motorcycle Boy was alone, living in a glass bubble and watching the world from it. What do you think he meant?

Short Answer Unit Test 2 *Rumble Fish*

V. Vocabulary

Listen to the vocabulary words and spell them. After you have spelled all the words, go back and write down the definitions.

WORD	**DEFINITION**
1. _____	_____
2. _____	_____
3. _____	_____
4. _____	_____
5. _____	_____
6. _____	_____
7. _____	_____
8. _____	_____
9. _____	_____
10. _____	_____

Vocabulary Part 2

Directions: Place the letter of the matching definition on the blank line.

_____ 1. allies   A. mocking
_____ 2. alternative   B. a period of time
_____ 3. atheist   C. a person who worships many gods
_____ 4. contrary   D. choice
_____ 5. era   E. a small amount of color
_____ 6. maniac   F. one who does not believe in God
_____ 7. pagan   G. supporters
_____ 8. rasping   H. a harsh, grating sound
_____ 9. sarcastic   I. opposite
_____ 10. tinge   J. madman

ANSWER KEY SHORT ANSWER UNIT TEST 2 *Rumble Fish*

I. <u>Matching/ Identify</u>

To the Teacher: Use this key for the Advanced Short Answer Unit Test as well.

D	1.	Cassandra	A.	owned the pet store
B	2.	Patty	B.	didn't like it when Rusty-James fought.
F	3.	Jeannie	C.	was expelled because of perfect semester tests.
I	4.	Mr. Harrigan	D.	liked the Motorcycle Boy.
A	5.	Mr. Donnely	E.	shot the Motorcycle Boy.
H	6.	Coach Ryan	F.	liked Steve but not Rusty-James.
E	7.	Patterson	G.	got out of the old neighborhood and went to college.
J	8.	Rusty-James	H.	wanted Rusty-James to beat up a student.
C	9.	the Motorcycle Boy	I.	was the school guidance counselor.
G	10.	Steve	J.	was suspended because of bad behavior.

II. <u>Short Answer</u>

1. Describe the fight with Biff. Include the way it ended.

    Biff wanted to fight because Rusty-James said something insulting to Anita. They met in an empty lot. Smokey, B. J., and Steve went with Rusty-James, although they said they would not fight. Biff had a knife and Rusty-James a bicycle chain. Rusty-James was able to get the knife away from Biff. The Motorcycle Boy arrived and Rusty got distracted. Biff cut him along the side. The Motorcycle Boy broke Biff's wrist. That ended the fight.

2. How did Rusty-James feel about his father? How did he feel about the Motorcycle Boy?

    He wasn't sure exactly how he felt. They got along okay, but didn't talk much. Rusty-James found it hard to respect his father, because he didn't do any work. He thought his father liked him more than he liked the Motorcycle Boy. He thought the Motorcycle Boy was the "coolest person in the world" and wanted to be just like him.

3. How did Rusty-James describe the feeling when the black guy hit him? How was Rusty-James saved?

    He said he was floating up in the air looking down at the others. It was like watching a movie. He heard the black guy say, "Killed him. Better get this one too." Then he saw his body laying on the alley floor. He knew he had to get back to his body, and a minute later he realized his head was hurting. The Motorcycle Boy came along and stopped the attack.

4. Describe the scene between Smokey and Rusty-James at Benny's.
   Patty came into Benny's. Smokey came in and sat with her. Rusty-James asked Smokey to step outside, and Smokey said he would not fight. They went outside and Rusty-James asked Smokey if he had planned for the news about the party to get back to Patty. Smokey said he did. Rusty-James said it was a smart thing to do, that he would not have thought of it.

5. Discuss the significance of the following quotation: "I can't remember much about it. Like I said, my memory's screwed up."
   Steve Hays recognized Rusty-James on the beach after they had not seen each other for about six years. Steve started talking about the old neighborhood. Rusty-James told him he did not remember much.

III. Fill in the Blank

1. When the story opened, Rusty-James was sitting on a beach. He had recently been released after spending five years in a **reformatory**.

2. Rusty-James did not have a very settled life. He and his older brother lived with their **father,** who drank most of the time.

3. Rusty and Biff **had a fight.**

4. There weren't any gangs anymore. The Motorcycle Boy said it was because **dope** had ruined them. Rusty-James missed them, and wanted them back.

5. Rusty-James continued to get into trouble. He was expelled from school, and his girlfriend, Patty **broke up with him.**

6. Smokey told Rusty-James he was not the **main tough guy**. The other boys would not follow him into a fight, because they thought he would get them killed.

7. Near the end of the story, Rusty-James followed his brother as he **broke into the pet store and released all of the animals**.

8. The Motorcycle Boy took the **Siamese fighting fish** to the river.

9. Rusty-James was behind his brother and heard the shot. He arrived to find **his brother was dead. He had been shot in the back.**

10. The story went back to the present. His old friend has asked him to meet for dinner. Rusty-James knew that he **would not** see his friend for dinner.

IV. Vocabulary Choose any ten words from the vocabulary lists to dictate for this section of the test.

Vocabulary Part 2
 Directions: Place the letter of the matching definition on the blank line.

G	1.	allies	A.	mocking
D	2.	alternative	B.	a period of time
F	3.	atheist	C.	a person who worships many gods
I	4.	contrary	D.	choice
B	5.	era	E.	a small amount of color
J	6.	maniac	F.	one who does not believe in God
C	7.	pagan	G.	supporters
H	8.	rasping	H.	a harsh, grating sound
A	9.	sarcastic	I.	opposite
E	10.	tinge	J.	madman

ADVANCED SHORT ANSWER UNIT TEST *Rumble Fish*

I. <u>Matching/Identify</u>

____ 1. Cassandra   A. owned the pet store
____ 2. Patty   B. didn't like it when Rusty-James fought.
____ 3. Jeannie   C. was expelled because of perfect semester tests.
____ 4. Mr. Harrigan   D. liked the Motorcycle Boy.
____ 5. Mr. Donnely   E. shot the Motorcycle Boy.
____ 6. Coach Ryan   F. liked Steve but not Rusty-James.
____ 7. Patterson   G. got out of the old neighborhood and went to college.
____ 8. Rusty-James   H. wanted Rusty-James to beat up a student.
____ 9. the Motorcycle Boy I. was the school guidance counselor.
____ 10. Steve   J. was suspended because of bad behavior.

II. <u>Short Answer</u>

1. Write a character sketch of one of the following: Steve Hays, Rusty-James, the Motorcycle Boy, the boys' father.

2. In Chapter 12, Steve tells Rusty-James that if he went back to the old neighborhood, it could give people heart attacks. Why?

Advanced Short Answer Unit Test *Rumble Fish*

3. Steve and Rusty-James are very different personalities. they seem unlikely as best friends. Why do you think Hinton included Steve's character, and made him the way he was?

4. What was the overall mood of the story? Give examples to support your answer.

5. Was the Motorcycle Boy's death necessary to the story? How would the outcome have changed if he had lived?

Advanced Short Answer Until Test *Rumble Fish*

III. <u>Quotations</u> Discuss the significance of the following quotations.

1. "You know who you look just like?"
   "Yeah," I said, and remembered everything. (Chapter 1)

2. "Kid," he said to me, "I never got past the river." (Chapter 3)

3. "Okay, let's get it straight what we're fighting for."
   "We're fighting to own this street."
   "Bull, We're fighting for fun." (Chapter 3)

105

Advanced Short Answer Unit Test *Rumble Fish*

4. "You know I don't steal things."
   "You know I *do*."

5. "It's a bit of a burden to be Robin Hood, Jesse James and the Pied Piper. I'd just as soon stay a neighborhood novelty, if it's all the same to you. It's not that I couldn't handle a larger scale, I just plain don't want to."

Advanced Short Answer Unit Test *Rumble Fish*

IV. Vocabulary

    Listen to the words and write them down. After you have written down all of the words, write a paragraph in which you use all of the words. The paragraph must in some way relate to *Rumblefish*.

1. _____
2. _____
3. _____
4. _____
5. _____

6. _____
7. _____
8. _____
9. _____
10. _____

_____
_____
_____
_____
_____
_____
_____
_____
_____
_____
_____

MULTIPLE CHOICE UNIT TEST 1 Rumble Fish

I. <u>Matching/ Identify</u>

____ 1. Cleveland   A. He didn't belong anywhere.
____ 2. loyalty   B. Steve's __ beat him for staying out late.
____ 3. California   C. It didn't scare Rusty-James.
____ 4. father   D. It was Rusty-James's only vice.
____ 5. Steve Hays   E. The Motorcycle Boy's ___ scared Rusty-James.
____ 6. the Motorcycle Boy   F. It was Biff's territory.
____ 7. mother   G. He spent five years in a reformatory.
____ 8. smile   H. He recognized his old friend on the beach.
____ 9. Rusty-James   I. The Motorcycle Boy went on a trip there.
____ 10. pain   J. Rusty-James's ___ left the family when he was two.

II. <u>Multiple Choice</u>

1. What literary device starts at the beginning of Chapter 2 and goes through Chapter 11?
    A. metaphor
    B. flashback
    C. hyperbole
    D. personification

2. What were Rusty-James's two main problems in Chapter 2?
    A. He was competing with the Motorcycle Boy to become the new gang leader, and the girl he liked didn't like him.
    B. He is failing in school and his mother has just left him and his brother alone and gone off with another man. .
    C. Biff Wilcox wants to fight him, and the Motorcycle Boy has not returned from his trip.
    D. His father has been missing for a week, and he doesn't have any money to buy food or pay the rent.

3. True or False: Smokey would have been the number one tough cat if it were not for Rusty-James.
    A. True
    B. False

Multiple Choice Unit Test 1 *Rumble Fish*

4. Which of the following statements about the Motorcycle Boy and Rusty-James is true?
   A. They are cousins.
   B. The Motorcycle Boy is nineteen and Rusty-James is sixteen.
   C. They both have blonde hair and green eyes.
   D. Rusty-James said the Motorcycle Boy looked like a panther.

5. How did Rusty-James feel about his father?
   A. Rusty-James found it hard to respect his father, because he didn't do any work.
   B. Rusty-James hated his father. He blamed him for losing his mother.
   C. Rusty-James loved his father and felt sorry for him.
   D. Rusty-James didn't care about his father at all.

6. How did Rusty-James feel about the Motorcycle Boy?
   A. He thought the Motorcycle Boy was "the coolest person in the world." He wanted to be just like him.
   B. He was jealous because the Motorcycle Boy got all of the attention.
   C. He thought the Motorcycle Boy was nuts, and didn't like to be around him.
   D. He thought the Motorcycle Boy acted stupid.

7. The Motorcycle Boy said it was fun at first, but then it got boring. What was he talking about?
   A. He was talking about dating Cassandra.
   B. He was talking about riding a motorcycle.
   C. He was talking about the gangs.
   D. He was talking about his life.

8. What scared Steve and Rusty-James about the Motorcycle Boy?
   A. They thought he was going to leave for good and forget about them.
   B. He said he had a gun and was going to use it soon.
   C. They thought he was going to go blind and deaf.
   D. He didn't belong anywhere, and didn't want to.

9. True or False: The Motorcycle Boy was shot and killed by Patterson, the policeman who had said he would get them.
   A. True
   B. False

Multiple Choice Unit Test 1 *Rumble Fish*

10. Was Rusty-James planning to meet Steve for dinner? What was his reason?
    A. Yes. He thought it would be good for him to connect with someone from his past who meant a lot to him.
    B. No. He did not want anyone he knew to find out what he used to be like.
    C. No. He thought if he did not see Steve, he could start forgetting again.
    D. Yes. He thought Steve might be able to help him remember some of the good times they had.

Multiple Choice Unit Test 1 *Rumble Fish*

III. <u>Quotations</u>   Write the letter of the word or phrase that completes the quotation.

1. "You know who you look just like?"

2. "You said you were going to quit fighting all the time."
   "Since when?"
   "Since you beat up Skip Handley. You promised me you wouldn't be fighting all the time."

3. "You know I don't steal things".

4. "Kid," he said to me, "I never. . . ."

5. "Russell-James," he said suddenly. "Are you ill?"
   "Got cut up in a knife fight," I told him."

6. "Apparently it is essential to some people. . ."

7. "It's a bit of a burden to be Robin Hood, Jesse James and the Pied Piper. I'd just as soon stay a neighbor-hood novelty, if it's all the same to you. . . "

8. "Rumble fish. . . "

9. "Hey, what's this? . . . "

10. ". . . right about that. I never thought you would, but you do. You don't sound like him, though. Your voice is completely different. . ."

A.   . . . got past the river."

B.   . . . It's not that I couldn't handle a larger scale, I just plain don't want to."

C.   . . . It's a good thing you never went back. You'd probably give half the people in the neighborhood a heart attack."

D.   . . . "Really?" He came over to take a look. "What strange lives you two lead."

E.   . . . "Yeah," I said, and remembered everything.

F.   . . . to belong--anywhere."

G.   . . . I thought we signed a treaty."

H.   . . . "Oh, yeah. Well, this ain't all the time. This is just once."

I.   . . . They'd kill each other if they could."

J.   . . . "You know I *do*." I answered.

Multiple Choice Unit Test 1 *Rumble Fish*

IV. Vocabulary Part 1 Place the letter of the matching definition on the blank line.

_____ 1. acute   A. difficult
_____ 2. complicated   B. offensive; annoying
_____ 3. distorted   C. permit; endure
_____ 4. innate   D. inherited; inborn
_____ 5. obnoxious   E. intense
_____ 6. perception   F. empty
_____ 7. simulated   G. imitation
_____ 8. tension   H. insight
_____ 9. tolerate   I. deformed; twisted out of shape
_____ 10. vacant   J. anxiety; unease

Vocabulary Part 2 Underline the word that matches the definition.

1. **alone**
   a. abandoned
   b. vacant
   c. solitary
   d. cautious

2. **bothered; annoyed**
   a. throbbing
   b. pestered
   c. contrary
   d. maniac

3. **mocking**
   a. obnoxious
   b. acute
   c. rasping
   d. sarcastic

4. **napping**
   a. dozing
   b. scowling
   c. stalking
   d. scrounging

5. **lively**
   a. superelite
   b. acute
   c. sassy
   d. maniac

6. **walking in an angry manner**
   a. obnoxious
   b. stalking
   c. throbbing
   d. scrounging

7. **a gang fight**
   a. era
   b. tension
   c. pagan
   d. rumble

8. **deserted; left**
   a. clipped
   b. pestered
   c. abandoned
   d. miscast

9. **in a confused manner**
   a. distorted
   b. pestered
   c. sarcastic
   d. dazedly

10. **hit with a sharp blow**
    a. clipped
    b. tinge
    c. complicated
    d. dozing

MULTIPLE CHOICE TEST 2 *Rumble Fish*

I. Matching/ Identify

___ 1.	Cassandra	A.	owned the pet store
___ 2.	Patty	B.	didn't like it when Rusty-James fought.
___ 3.	Jeannie	C.	was expelled because of perfect semester tests.
___ 4.	Mr. Harrigan	D.	liked the Motorcycle Boy.
___ 5.	Mr. Donnely	E.	shot the Motorcycle Boy.
___ 6.	Coach Ryan	F.	liked Steve but not Rusty-James.
___ 7.	Patterson	G.	got out of the old neighborhood and went to college.
___ 8.	Rusty-James	H.	wanted Rusty-James to beat up a student.
___ 9.	the Motorcycle Boy	I.	was the school guidance counselor.
___ 10.	Steve	J.	was suspended because of bad behavior.

II. Multiple Choice

1. Where was Rusty-James when the story opened?
    A. He was in a hospital.
    B. He was in school.
    C. He was on a beach.
    D. He was in a prison.

2. True or False: Steve and the others were glad Rusty-James was going to fight. They said there had not been enough action lately.
    A. True
    B. False

3. Rusty-James was upset that Biff was violating the rules. How was Biff doing this?
    A. Biff had a knife and had not told him about it before the fight.
    B. Biff had brought more friends than he said he would, so the sides were not even.
    C. Biff had a gun, and the gangs had agreed not to use guns.
    D. Biff got to the empty lot early and booby-trapped it.

4. What did Steve say the difference between the Motorcycle Boy and Rusty-James was?
    A. He said the Motorcycle Boy acted, but Rusty-James only bragged.
    B. He said Rusty-James cared about people, but the Motorcycle Boy didn't.
    C. He could tell what Rusty-James was thinking, but not what the Motorcycle Boy was thinking.
    D. He said the Motorcycle Boy was tough, but Rusty-James only acted tough.

Multiple Choice Test 2 *Rumble Fish*

5. Which of the following did **not** happen in the scene with the Chevy?
    A. Rusty-James took the mag wheels off the car.
    B. They jumped from one roof to another to get away from the guys who were chasing them.
    C. After they got across, Steve told Rusty-James he should not have stolen the hubcaps, but Rusty-James ignored him.
    D. On the way home, Steve said he would report Rusty-James to the police if he ever tried to steal again.

6. How did Rusty-James feel about his father?
    A. Rusty-James found it hard to respect his father, because he didn't do any work.
    B. Rusty-James hated his father. He blamed him for losing his mother.
    C. Rusty-James loved his father and felt sorry for him.
    D. Rusty-James didn't care about his father at all.

7. What happened when Rusty-James saw Patty at the bus stop?
    A. She told him she loved him.
    B. She hit him and broke his nose.
    C. She broke up with him.
    D. She invited him to go home with her.

8. Which of the following is **not** part of the way Rusty-James described the attack on him?
    A. The two guys asked for money.
    B. Rusty-James said he was floating up in the air looking down at the others.
    C. He heard the black guy say, "Killed him. Better get this one too."
    D. He felt someone on the ground pull his mind back into his body.

9. What did Rusty-James tell Steve he wanted the two of them to do?
    A. Rusty-James wanted the two of them to get an apartment together.
    B. Rusty-James wanted to follow the Motorcycle Boy around for a few days.
    C. Rusty-James wanted Steve to transfer to Cleveland High with him.
    D. Rusty-James wanted Steve to help him rob the drugstore.

10. Rusty-James asked his father about his mother. Which of the following statements was **not** part of his father's answer?
    A. His father said she had married him for fun, and when the fun stopped she left.
    B. His father said his mother was crazy.
    C. He said she had a different view of the world
    D. He said he married her to set a precedent.

Multiple Choice Test 2 *Rumble Fish*

III. Quotations   Write the letter of the word or phrase that completes the quotation.

1. "Lookit, me an' Biff'll settle this thing ourselves. . . "

2. "Russell-James," he said suddenly. "Are you ill?"
"Got cut up in a knife fight," I told him."

3. "I think," he said thoughtfully,. . . "

4. "Don't you think it's time. . . "

5. "That was pretty good," said the Motorcycle Boy. "Did you ever think of trying out for a chameleon?"

6. "My, my, my. Ain't he fine?"

7. "What a funny situation. I wonder what I'm doing here, holding my half-dead brother, surrounded by bricks and cement and rats.

8. "I've tried to help you. But I've got to think about myself some. . ."

9. ". . . right about that. I never thought you would, but you do. You don't sound like him, though. Your voice is completely different. . ."

10. I was so scared I dropped my head down on the counter . . ."

A. . . . "Really?" He came over to take a look. "What strange lives you two lead."

B. . . . "I don't know them," I said, kind of proud of myself. "Where's their turf?"

C. . . . Although I suppose it's a s good a place to be as any. There weren't so many walls in California, but if you're used to walls all that air can give you the creeps."

D. . . . You're just like a ball in a pinball machine. Getting slammed back and forth; and you never think about anything, about where you're going or how to get there. "

E. . . . "Yeah. And I'm gonna look just like him."

F. . . . You guys'll just be an audience, huh? Ain't nothin' wrong with an audience."

G. . . . and cried for the first time I could remember. Crying hurts like hell."

H. . . . you gave some serious thought to your life?"

I. . . . It's a good thing you never went back. You'd probably give half the people in the neighborhood a heart attack."

J. . . . that the show is over."

Multiple Choice Test 2 *Rumble Fish*

IV. <u>Vocabulary Part 1</u>   Match the word and the definition.

____ 1. allies   A. mocking
____ 2. alternative   B. a period of time
____ 3. atheist   C. a person who worships many gods
____ 4. contrary   D. choice
____ 5. era   E. a small amount of color
____ 6. maniac   F. one who does not believe in God
____ 7. pagan   G. supporters
____ 8. rasping   H. a harsh, grating sound
____ 9. sarcastic   I. opposite
____ 10. tinge   J. madman

<u>Vocabulary Part 2</u> Write the letter of the word that matches the definition.

1. **put in an unsuitable roll**
   a. abandoned
   b. vacant
   c. miscast
   d. cautious

2. **insight**
   a. tinge
   b. era
   c. cautious
   d. perception

3. **mocking**
   a. obnoxious
   b. acute
   c. rasping
   d. sarcastic

4. **napping**
   a. dozing
   b. scowling
   c. stalking
   d. scrounging

5. **lively**
   a. superelite
   b. acute
   c. sassy
   d. maniac

6. **aching**
   a. vacant
   b. throbbing
   c. rasping
   d. acute

7. **uncivilized**
   a. era
   b. tension
   c. pagan
   d. primitive

8. **example for future actions**
   a. atheist
   b. precedent
   c. pagan
   d. precedent

9. **difficult; involved**
   a. scrounging
   b. complicated
   c. contrary
   d. simulated

10. **permit; endure**
    a. tolerate
    b. contrary
    c. tinge
    d. simulated

ANSWER SHEET Multiple Choice Unit Tests *Rumblef Fsh*

I. Matching

1. ____
2. ____
3. ____
4. ____
5. ____
6. ____
7. ____
8. ____
9. ____
10. ____

II. Multiple Choice

1. (A) (B) (C) (D)
2. (A) (B) (C) (D)
3. (A) (B) (C) (D)
4. (A) (B) (C) (D)
5. (A) (B) (C) (D)
6. (A) (B) (C) (D)
7. (A) (B) (C) (D)
8. (A) (B) (C) (D)
9. (A) (B) (C) (D)
10. (A) (B) (C) (D)

III. Quotations

1. ____
2. ____
3. ____
4. ____
5. ____
6. ____
7. ____
8. ____
9. ____
10. ____

IV. Vocabulary Part 1

1. ____
2. ____
3. ____
4. ____
5. ____
6. ____
7. ____
8. ____
9. ____
10. ____

Vocabulary Part 2

1. ____
2. ____
3. ____
4. ____
5. ____
6. ____
7. ____
8. ____
9. ____
10. ____

ANSWER SHEET KEY Multiple Choice Unit Test 1 *Rumble Fish*

I. Matching	III. Quotations	IV. Vocabulary Part 1
1. F	1. E	1. E
2. D	2. H	2. A
3. I	3. J	3. I
4. B	4. A	4. D
5. H	5. D	5. B
6. A	6. F	6. H
7. J	7. B	7. G
8. E	8. I	8. J
9. G	9. G	9. C
10. C	10. C	10. F

Vocabulary Part 2

II. Multiple Choice

1. (A) ( ) (C) (D)
2. (A) (B) ( ) (D)
3. ( ) (B) (C) (D)
4. (A) (B) (C) ( )
5. ( ) (B) (C) (D)
6. ( ) (B) (C) (D)
7. (A) (B) ( ) (D)
8. (A) (B) (C) ( )
9. ( ) (B) (C) (D)
10. (A) (B) ( ) (D)

11. C
12. B
13. D
14. A
15. C
16. B
17. D
18. C
19. D
20. A

ANSWER SHEET KEY Multiple Choice Unit Test 2 *Rumble Fish*

I. Matching

1. D
2. B
3. F
4. I
5. A
6. H
7. E
8. J
9. C
10. G

II. Multiple Choice

1. (A) (B) ( ) (D)
2. (A) ( ) (C) (D)
3. ( ) (B) (C) (D)
4. (A) (B) ( ) (D)
5. (A) (B) (C) ( )
6. ( ) (B) (C) (D)
7. (A) (B) ( ) (D)
8. (A) (B) (C) ( )
9. (A) ( ) (C) (D)
10. (A) ( ) (C) (D)

III. Quotations

1. F
2. A
3. J
4. H
5. B
6. E
7. C
8. D
9. I
10. G

IV. Vocabulary Part 1

1. G
2. D
3. F
4. I
5. B
6. J
7. C
8. H
9. A
10. E

Vocabulary Part 2

1. C
2. D
3. D
4. A
5. C
6. B
7. D
8. B
9. B
10. A

UNIT RESOURCE MATERIALS

BULLETIN BOARD IDEAS *Rumble Fish*

1. Save one corner of the board for the best of students' *Rumble Fish* writing assignments.

2. Take one of the word search puzzles from the extra activities packet and with a marker copy it over in a large size on the bulletin board. Write the clue words to find to one side. Invite students prior to and after class to find the words and circle them on the bulletin board.

3. Have students find or draw pictures that they think resemble the people in the book and put them together into a collage.

4. Invite students to help make an interactive bulletin board quiz. Give each student a half-sheet of paper folded in half so that it can open. On the outside flap, have each student write a description of one of the characters in the text. On the inside, they will write the name of the character. You can staple or tack these papers to the bulletin board so that the students can read the descriptions and lift the flaps to find the answers.

5. Collect pictures of the area mentioned in the book.

6. Display articles about *Rumble Fish* or S. E. Hinton.

7. Collect and display newspaper and magazine articles about teenagers in the city, or gang activities.

EXTRA ACTIVITIES *Rumble Fish*

One of the difficulties in teaching a novel is that all students don't read at the same speed. One student who likes to read may take the book home and finish it in a day or two. Sometimes a few students finish the in-class assignments early. The problem, then, is finding suitable extra activities for students.

One thing that helps is to keep a little library in the classroom. For this unit on *Rumble Fish* you might check out from the school or public library other books by S. E. Hinton. There are also many other related novels that students would enjoy reading. Several journals have critiques of Hinton's works. Some of the students may enjoy reading these and responding either in writing or in discussion groups.

Your students who have reading difficulties, or speak English as a second language may benefit from listening to all or part of the book on tape. This is available commercially, or your better readers could make one for class use.

Other things you may keep on hand are word search puzzles. Several puzzles relating directly to *Rumble Fish* are included in the unit. Feel free to duplicate them.

Some students may like to draw. You might devise a contest or allow some extra-credit grade for students who draw characters or scenes from *Rumble Fish.* Note, too, that if the students do not want to keep their drawings you may pick up some extra bulletin board materials this way. If you have a contest and you supply the prize. You could, possibly, make the drawing itself a non-refundable entry fee.

Have maps, a globe, and travel brochures on hand for easy reference. Travel agencies and automobile clubs are good sources for these materials. Students can plot a trip from their home town to California.

The pages which follow contain games, puzzles, and worksheets. The keys, when appropriate, immediately follow the puzzle or worksheet. There are two main groups of activities: one group for the unit; that is, generally relating to the *Rumblefish* text, and another group of activities related strictly to the *Rumble Fish* vocabulary.

Directions for the games, puzzles, and worksheets are self-explanatory. The object here is to provide you with extra materials you may use in any way you choose.

MORE ACTIVITIES *Rumble Fish*

To the Teacher: Any of these activities could be used as an additional or alternative assessment.

1. Pick one of the incidents to dramatize. Write dialogue for the characters. (Perhaps you could assign various stories to different groups of students so more than one part of the story could be acted and more students could participate.)

2. Design a book cover (front and back and inside flaps) for *Rumble Fish*. The front flap should contain a synopsis of the plot. The back flap should have a short character sketch and a review of the book. The cover should have a drawing of a key scene from the book.

3. Design a bulletin board (ready to be put up; not just sketched) for *Rumble Fish*.

4. Invite a story teller to tell one or more stories related to *Rumble Fish* to the class.

5. Use some of the related topics (noted earlier for an in-class library) as topics for research, reports, or written papers, or as topics for guest speakers.

6. Design and produce a talk show. Choose one of the story incidents as the topic. The host will interview the various characters. (Students should make up the questions they want the host to ask the characters.)

7. Work in pairs to create an interview with one of the characters. One student should be the interviewer and the other should be the interviewee. Students can work together to compose questions for the interviewer to ask. Each pair of students could present their interview to the class.

8. Invite students who have read other books by S. E. Hinton to present booktalks to the class.

9. Hold small group discussions related to topics in the book. Assign a recorder and a speaker for each group. Have the speaker from each group make a report to the class.

10. Invite students who have read a biography of S. E. Hinton to tell the class about her life.

11. Write a sequel telling what happened to Rusty-James after he met Steve on the beach.

12. Write a letter to Rusty-James and try to convince him to change his lifestyle.

13. Write a letter from Rusty-James's mother explaining why she left the family.

14. Keep a reading response journal while reading the novel.

15. Write a review of the novel.

16. Write a newspaper article based on an event from the novel. Individuals could choose different events and assemble their stories into a Rumble Fish newspaper.

17. Make a poster designed to advertise the novel to other students.

18. Make a diorama showing one of the scenes from the book.

19. Make a mobile showing the main characters and setting. Write a description on the back of each piece.

20. Make a comic book version of the story to share with younger readers.

21. Create a Readers' Theater play based on a scene or chapter from the novel.

22. Write a different ending for the story.

23. Create a radio or television commercial to advertise the book.

24. Make a timeline showing important events from the story.

25. Retell the story from another point of view (the Motorcycle Boy, Steve, Officer Patterson, Patty, one of the parents.)

Rumble Fish Word Search

```
S M O K E Y P Y C A L I F O R N I A Y
I P B H X R V J J I C L R F Y Q L Z F
A A D H N E V V V S H X V H R M I N G
M T N V H H D E F Q B Z T N O C T D L
E T Q C A R D N A S S A C A T L P L L
S E F B G E N I Z A G A M G A E L T W
E R L V D J L V Y S A K R I M V E M M
L S G Y O T E G D I M X Q R R E A B H
P O B B N N Z Y K H E L Q R O L N E M
P N Y Q N J X T W Y V Z E A F A I N M
A F T A E B A I H H E H M H E N T N X
C T B E L C Y C R O T O M J R D A Y G
K K T I Y T A Q K O S C C E R P K T Q
E X N P B E Y M R S Z H Y A D A N T Y
R D A T B I P B D P O W Z N E R I A N
S I N A Y R F O O R A N Q N M R F P H
N O B N L M P F B L R X S I I O E B Q
D H S I F E L B M U R P R E L T Y Z J
H O S P I T A L S M I L E V K S H O T
```

ANITA	DON	MAGS	RUMBLEFISH
BEACH	DONNELY	MIDGET	RYAN
BENNY	DOPE	MILK	SHOT
BIFF	HARRIGAN	MOTORCYCLE	SIAMESE
BLIND	HOSPITAL	PACKERS	SIN
BROTHER	JACKSON	PAIN	SMILE
CALIFORNIA	JEANNIE	PARROT	SMOKEY
CASSANDRA	KNIFE	PATTERSON	SNEAKY
CHEVY	LAWYER	PATTY	STEVE
CITY	LITTLE	PET	
CLEVELAND	LOYALTY	REFORMATORY	
DEVIL	MAGAZINE	ROOF	

Rumble Fish Word Search

```
S M O K E Y   Y C A L I F O R N I A
I P       V     I         Y     L
A A       E   V           R     I
M T       H     E       N O C   T
E T     C A R D N A S S A C A T L T
S E       E N I Z A G A M G A   L E
E R     D         A     I M V   E
L S     O T E G D I M   R R E A B
    O     N     Y     E   O L N E
P N Y     N J   T   V   E A I   N
A   A   E B A I H   E H   H N T   N
C   E L C Y C R O T O M J R D A Y
K   I Y T A   K O S       E P K T
E N P B E Y   R       Y   A N T
R D A B I   B D   O W   N E R I A
S I N A Y R F O O R A N   N M R F P
N O       P F   L     S I I O E
D H S I F E L B M U R     E L T
H O S P I T A L S M I L E   K S H O T
```

ANITA	DON	MAGS	RUMBLEFISH
BEACH	DONNELY	MIDGET	RYAN
BENNY	DOPE	MILK	SHOT
BIFF	HARRIGAN	MOTORCYCLE	SIAMESE
BLIND	HOSPITAL	PACKERS	SIN
BROTHER	JACKSON	PAIN	SMILE
CALIFORNIA	JEANNIE	PARROT	SMOKEY
CASSANDRA	KNIFE	PATTERSON	SNEAKY
CHEVY	LAWYER	PATTY	STEVE
CITY	LITTLE	PET	
CLEVELAND	LOYALTY	REFORMATORY	
DEVIL	MAGAZINE	ROOF	

Rumble Fish Crossword

Across
1. Rusty-James drank it a lot: ___ Pete
3. Rusty-James jumped from one to another
4. Would have been the top tough guy
7. Knifed Rusty-James: ___ Wilcox
9. Student teacher who liked the Motorcycle Boy
13. Coach wanted Rusty-James to beat him up
14. It didn't scare Rusty-James
15. The Motorcycle Boy broke into it: ___ store
16. Where the story started
19. Rusty-James liked the excitement there
20. Junior high hangout: ____'s
21. Rusty-James drank it before a fight: chocolate ___
23. Would have been Biff's gang: ___ Hawks
24. The Motorcycle Boy died from it
25. The hubcaps Rusty-James tried to steal
26. Pet store owner
27. Tallest boy in the crowd

Down
1. The Motorcycle Boy took the ___ fish to the river
2. Rusty-James insulted her
3. Coach who wanted Rusty-James to beat up a student
5. It had a picture of Motorcycle Boy
6. Bill's weapon
8. It said a lot of bad words
9. The car with mag wheels
10. Steve didn't like the movies there: ___ City
11. It ruined the gangs.
12. ____ Boy didn't belong anywhere
15. Local gang
16. The Motorcycle Boy's condition: color ___
17. School Rusty-James did not want to attend
18. The Motorcycle Boy's scared Rusty-James
22. Rusty-James's girlfriend

Rumble Fish Crossword Answer Key

	1 S	N	2 E	A	K	Y					3 R	O	O	F
	I		N				4	5		6				
								S	M	O	K	E	Y	
	A		7 B	I	F	F			A		N		A	
	M		T			8 P			G		I		N	
	E		9 C	10 A	S	S	A	11 N	D	R	A		F		12 M
	S		H	I		R		O		Z		E	13 D	O	N
	E			N		R		14 P	A	I	N			T	
				V				O		E		N			O	
					15 P	E	T		16 B	E	17 A	C	H		R
					A				L		L				C
	18 S		19 C	I	T	Y			I		20 B	E	N	N	Y
	21 M	I	L	K					N		E		V		C
	I			E			22 P		23 D	E	V	I	L		
	L			R			A				L		E		
	E			24 S	H	O	T		25 M	A	G	S			
							T				N				
	26 D	O	N	N	E	L	Y		27 M	I	D	G	E	T	

Across
1. Rusty-James drank it a lot: ___ Pete
3. Rusty-James jumped from one to another
4. Would have been the top tough guy
7. Knifed Rusty-James: ___ Wilcox
9. Student teacher who liked the Motorcycle Boy
13. Coach wanted Rusty-James to beat him up
14. It didn't scare Rusty-James
15. The Motorcycle Boy broke into it: ___ store
16. Where the story started
19. Rusty-James liked the excitement there
20. Junior high hangout: ____'s
21. Rusty-James drank it before a fight: chocolate ___
23. Would have been Biff's gang: ___ Hawks
24. The Motorcycle Boy died from it
25. The hubcaps Rusty-James tried to steal
26. Pet store owner
27. Tallest boy in the crowd

Down
1. The Motorcycle Boy took the ___ fish to the river
2. Rusty-James insulted her
3. Coach who wanted Rusty-James to beat up a student
5. It had a picture of Motorcycle Boy
6. Bill's weapon
8. It said a lot of bad words
9. The car with mag wheels
10. Steve didn't like the movies there: ___ City
11. It ruined the gangs.
12. ____ Boy didn't belong anywhere
15. Local gang
16. The Motorcycle Boy's condition: color ___
17. School Rusty-James did not want to attend
18. The Motorcycle Boy's scared Rusty-James
22. Rusty-James's girlfriend

MATCHING QUIZ/WORKSHEET 1 - Rumble Fish

___ 1. CALIFORNIA   A. Student teacher who liked the Motorcycle Boy

___ 2. BLIND   B. Tallest boy in the crowd

___ 3. PACKERS   C. Police officer who shot the Motorcycle Boy

___ 4. MOTORCYCLE   D. Guidance counselor

___ 5. HARRIGAN   E. Rusty-James drank it a lot: ___ Pete

___ 6. KNIFE   F. Would have been Biff's gang: ___ Hawks

___ 7. PATTERSON   G. It had a picture of Motorcycle Boy

___ 8. RUMBLEFISH   H. The Motorcycle Boy went there

___ 9. LAWYER   I. Steve's mother was there

___ 10. MIDGET   J. Local gang

___ 11. HOSPITAL   K. The Motorcycle Boy's scared Rusty-James

___ 12. DEVIL   L. Pet store owner

___ 13. PAIN   M. Rusty-James's only vice

___ 14. SHOT   N. Rusty-James's father was an ex-____ who drank all day

___ 15. MAGS   O. Rusty-James spent five years there

___ 16. REFORMATORY   P. ____ Boy didn't belong anywhere

___ 17. DONNELY   Q. The hubcaps Rusty-James tried to steal

___ 18. ROOF   R. It didn't scare Rusty-James

___ 19. MAGAZINE   S. The Motorcycle Boy died from it

___ 20. SMILE   T. Rusty-James jumped from one to another

___ 21. DOPE   U. Would have been the top tough guy

___ 22. SMOKEY   V. It ruined the gangs.

___ 23. CASSANDRA   W. Siamese fighting fish that killed each other

___ 24. LOYALTY   X. The Motorcycle Boy's condition: color ___

___ 25. SNEAKY   Y. Bill's weapon

KEY: MATCHING QUIZ/WORKSHEET 1 - Rumble Fish

H - 1.	CALIFORNIA	A. Student teacher who liked the Motorcycle Boy
X - 2.	BLIND	B. Tallest boy in the crowd
J - 3.	PACKERS	C. Police officer who shot the Motorcycle Boy
P - 4.	MOTORCYCLE	D. Guidance counselor
D - 5.	HARRIGAN	E. Rusty-James drank it a lot: ___ Pete
Y - 6.	KNIFE	F. Would have been Biff's gang: ___ Hawks
C - 7.	PATTERSON	G. It had a picture of Motorcycle Boy
W 8.	RUMBLEFISH	H. The Motorcycle Boy went there
N - 9.	LAWYER	I. Steve's mother was there
B -10.	MIDGET	J. Local gang
I - 11.	HOSPITAL	K. The Motorcycle Boy's scared Rusty-James
F -12.	DEVIL	L. Pet store owner
R -13.	PAIN	M. Rusty-James's only vice
S -14.	SHOT	N. Rusty-James's father was an ex-____ who drank all day
Q -15.	MAGS	O. Rusty-James spent five years there
O -16.	REFORMATORY	P. ____ Boy didn't belong anywhere
L -17.	DONNELY	Q. The hubcaps Rusty-James tried to steal
T -18.	ROOF	R. It didn't scare Rusty-James
G -19.	MAGAZINE	S. The Motorcycle Boy died from it
K -20.	SMILE	T. Rusty-James jumped from one to another
V -21.	DOPE	U. Would have been the top tough guy
U -22.	SMOKEY	V. It ruined the gangs.
A -23.	CASSANDRA	W. Siamese fighting fish that killed each other
M 24.	LOYALTY	X. The Motorcycle Boy's condition: color ___
E -25.	SNEAKY	Y. Bill's weapon

MATCHING QUIZ/WORKSHEET 2 - Rumble Fish

___ 1. SNEAKY   A. Rusty-James drank it before a fight: chocolate ___

___ 2. CITY   B. Junior high hangout: ____'s

___ 3. RYAN   C. Guidance counselor

___ 4. MILK   D. Where the story started

___ 5. HARRIGAN   E. The car with mag wheels

___ 6. MAGS   F. Rusty-James's best friend

___ 7. SIAMESE   G. Steve's mother was there

___ 8. SMILE   H. School Rusty-James did not want to attend

___ 9. MOTORCYCLE   I. The Motorcycle Boy took the ___ fish to the river

___ 10. MAGAZINE   J. Pee-wee branch of the local gang: ___ Leaguers

___ 11. BEACH   K. It had a picture of Motorcycle Boy

___ 12. LITTLE   L. It didn't scare Rusty-James

___ 13. STEVE   M. Rusty-James liked the excitement there

___ 14. KNIFE   N. Police officer who shot the Motorcycle Boy

___ 15. CHEVY   O. It said a lot of bad words

___ 16. CLEVELAND   P. Pet store owner

___ 17. HOSPITAL   Q. Coach who wanted Rusty-James to beat up a student

___ 18. PAIN   R. Student teacher who liked the Motorcycle Boy

___ 19. CASSANDRA   S. ____ Boy didn't belong anywhere

___ 20. BENNY   T. Rusty-James drank it a lot: ___ Pete

___ 21. DEVIL   U. The hubcaps Rusty-James tried to steal

___ 22. PARROT   V. Bill's weapon

___ 23. PACKERS   W. Local gang

___ 24. PATTERSON   X. Would have been Biff's gang: ___ Hawks

___ 25. DONNELY   Y. The Motorcycle Boy's scared Rusty-James

KEY: MATCHING QUIZ/WORKSHEET 2 - Rumble Fish

T - 1. SNEAKY	A. Rusty-James drank it before a fight: chocolate ___
M - 2. CITY	B. Junior high hangout: ___'s
Q - 3. RYAN	C. Guidance counselor
A - 4. MILK	D. Where the story started
C - 5. HARRIGAN	E. The car with mag wheels
U - 6. MAGS	F. Rusty-James's best friend
I - 7. SIAMESE	G. Steve's mother was there
Y - 8. SMILE	H. School Rusty-James did not want to attend
S - 9. MOTORCYCLE	I. The Motorcycle Boy took the ___ fish to the river
K -10. MAGAZINE	J. Pee-wee branch of the local gang: ___ Leaguers
D -11. BEACH	K. It had a picture of Motorcycle Boy
J -12. LITTLE	L. It didn't scare Rusty-James
F -13. STEVE	M. Rusty-James liked the excitement there
V -14. KNIFE	N. Police officer who shot the Motorcycle Boy
E -15. CHEVY	O. It said a lot of bad words
H -16. CLEVELAND	P. Pet store owner
G -17. HOSPITAL	Q. Coach who wanted Rusty-James to beat up a student
L -18. PAIN	R. Student teacher who liked the Motorcycle Boy
R -19. CASSANDRA	S. ___ Boy didn't belong anywhere
B -20. BENNY	T. Rusty-James drank it a lot: ___ Pete
X -21. DEVIL	U. The hubcaps Rusty-James tried to steal
O -22. PARROT	V. Bill's weapon
W 23. PACKERS	W. Local gang
N -24. PATTERSON	X. Would have been Biff's gang: ___ Hawks
P -25. DONNELY	Y. The Motorcycle Boy's scared Rusty-James

JUGGLE WORDS *Rumble Fish*

JUGGLE	WORD	CLUE
NTAIA	ANITA	Rusty-James insulted her
AKJSBOCN	B. J. JACKSON	fat, but tough
ECAHB	BEACH	where the story started
SENYBN	BENNY'S	junior high hangout
FIFWXIBCOL	BIFF WILCOX	knifed Rusty-James
FOLRNAIACI	CALIFORNIA	The Motorcycle Boy went there.
SACANDRAS	CASSANDRA	student teacher who liked the Motorcycle Boy
CEYHV	CHEVY	the car with mag wheels
HOLMATEILKCOC	CHOCOLATE MILK	Rusty-James drank it before a fight
YICT	CITY	Rusty-James like the excitement there.
VLCLANEDE	CLEVELAND	Rusty-James did not want to go to this school.
ROCYANCAH	COACH RYAN	wanted Rusty-James to beat up a student
LOBLONRDCI	COLOR BLIND	the Motorcycle boy's condition
WEILSDHAKV	DEVIL HAWKS	It would have been Biff's gang.
EONPPRI	DON PRICE	Coach wanted Rusty-James to beat him up.
POED	DOPE	It ruined the gangs.
REANIJEMNANTI	JEANNIE MARTIN	She liked Steve but not Rusty-James.
NIEKF	KNIFE	Biff's weapon
ITTAELEGERSLLU	LITTLE LEAGUERS	pee-wee branch of the local gang
OLATYLY	LOYALTY	It was Rusty James's only vice.
NELYNOD	DONNELY	pet store owner
AZAINEMG	MAGAZINE	It had a picture of the Motorcycle Boy.
SAGM	MAGS	the hubcaps Rusty-James tried to steal
GIDETM	MIDGET	tallest boy in the crowd
RHIGAANR	HARRIGAN	Guidance Counselor
OYTBRMCLEOOYC	MOTORCYCLE BOY	didn't belong anywhere
AERCSPK	PACKERS	local gang
AIPN	PAIN	It didn't scare Rusty-James.
AROPTR	PARROT	It said a lot of bad words.
SATEROPNT	PATTERSON	police officer who shot the Motorcycle Boy
PTYAT	PATTY	Rusty-James's girlfriend
ESOTREPT	PET STORE	the Motorcycle Boy broke into it
EFRRRYMAOTO	REFORMATORY	Rusty-James spent five years there.
OFOR	ROOF	Rusty-James jumped from one to another
BLREUFISHM	RUMBLEFISH	Siamese fighting fish that killed each other
ARTHFE	FATHER	ex-lawyer: drank all day
UTYJMESSAR	RUSTY-JAME	wants to be like his brother
MORETH	MOTHER	left the family and went to California

OTHS	SHOT	The Motorcycle Boy died from it.
INYCITS	SIN CITY	Steve didn't like the movies there.
MIELS	SMILE	The Motorcycle Boy's scared Rusty-James.
MYSOEK	SMOKEY	would have been the top tough guy
NEKYEPETAS	SNEAKY PETE	Rusty-James drank it a lot
TVEHSSAYE	STEVE HAYS	Rusty-James's best friend

VOCABULARY RESOURCE MATERIALS

Rumble Fish Vocabulary Word Search

```
R N T S C O W L I N G V A C A N T P Y
A O O O L A P L B Q M G L H T V S K H
S V L L I Z U P M X Q A Y D T X A H Q
P E E I P N H T G N I G N U O R C S Q
I L R T P A N S I Y N H A I R Z S S C
N T A A E J B A U O Z D G X A V I O S
G Y T R D W N A T P U P A G V C M N G
Y C E Y L Y N Y N E E S P B T P J S G
S I M U L A T E D D Z R Y G L N Y A N
D P P E R C E P T I O N E I L V G R I
I T R Y K B T G Y A N N C L G X D C B
S E I E M M U B Y T K A E P I J A A B
T N M V C X C S D H T X M D D T Z S O
O S I Y D E A L T E R N A T I V E T R
R I T K L S D V D I R Y B B Q I D I H
T O I Z S B D E F S C A V M L D L C T
E N V Y H E V E N T U A L L Y G Y B C
D P E S T E R E D T S T A L K I N G Q
C O N T R A R Y L V T T I N G E D F L
```

ABANDONED	CONTRARY	MISCAST	SARCASTIC	TENSION
ACUTE	DAZEDLY	NOVELTY	SASSY	THROBBING
ALLIES	DISTORTED	PAGAN	SCOWLING	TINGE
ALTERNATIVE	DOZING	PERCEPTION	SCROUNGING	TOLERATE
ATHEIST	ERA	PESTERED	SIMULATED	VACANT
CAUTIOUS	EVENTUALLY	PRECEDENT	SOLITARY	
CLIPPED	INNATE	PRIMITIVE	STALKING	
COMPLICATED	MANIAC	RASPING	SUPERELITE	

Rumble Fish Vocabulary Word Search Answer Key

```
R  N  T  S  C  O  W  L  I  N  G  V  A  C  A  N  T
A  O  O  O  L  A           M              S
S  V  L  L  I     U           A     D        A
P  E  E  I  P  N     T  G  N  I  G  N  U  O  R  C  S
I  L  R  T  P  A  N  S  I        A     I  Z     C
N  T  A  A  E     B  A  U  O        G     A  I  O
G  Y  T  R  D     A  T  P  U        A     C  M  N
      E  Y        N  E  E  S  P           P  S  G
S  I  M  U  L  A  T  E  D  D     R        L     A  N
D  P  P  E  R  C  E  P  T  I  O  N  E  I        R  I
I  T  R        T        A     N  C  L        D  C  B
S  E  I  E     U        T     A  E     I     A  A  B
T  N  M     C     C  S     H  T     D     T  Z  S  O
O  S  I        E  A  L  T  E  R  N  A  T  I  V  E  T  R
R  I  T        S  D     D  I  R                 I  D  I  H
T  O  I        S        E     S     A        L     L  C  T
E  N  V  Y     E  V  E  N  T  U  A  L  L  Y        Y
D  P  E  S  T  E  R  E  D     T  S  T  A  L  K  I  N  G
C  O  N  T  R  A  R  Y              T  I  N  G  E
```

ABANDONED	CONTRARY	MISCAST	SARCASTIC	TENSION
ACUTE	DAZEDLY	NOVELTY	SASSY	THROBBING
ALLIES	DISTORTED	PAGAN	SCOWLING	TINGE
ALTERNATIVE	DOZING	PERCEPTION	SCROUNGING	TOLERATE
ATHEIST	ERA	PESTERED	SIMULATED	VACANT
CAUTIOUS	EVENTUALLY	PRECEDENT	SOLITARY	
CLIPPED	INNATE	PRIMITIVE	STALKING	
COMPLICATED	MANIAC	RASPING	SUPERELITE	

Rumble Fish Vocabulary Crossword

Across
1. Intense
3. Empty
11. Insight
12. A period of time
14. Inherited; inborn
15. Anxiety; unease
17. Lively
21. Walking in an angry manner
23. Difficult; involved
25. Person who worships many gods
26. Uncivilized; simple
27. Permit; endure

Down
2. Hit with a sharp blow
4. Supporters; partners
5. Deserted; left
6. Small amount of color
7. Napping
8. Example for future actions
9. Bothered; annoyed
10. Opposite
13. Harsh, grating sound
16. New and unusual thing
18. Imitation
19. Mocking
20. Put in an unsuitable role
22. One who does not believe in God
24. Madman; lunatic

Rumble Fish Vocabulary Crossword Answer Key

				¹A	²C	U	T	E			³V	⁴A	C	⁵A	N	⁶T	
					L							L		B		I	
⁷D					I		⁸P		⁹P			L		A		N	
O		¹⁰C		¹¹P	E	R	C	E	P	T	I	O	N			G	
Z		O		P			E		E			E		D		¹²E	¹³R	A
¹⁴I	N	N	A	T	E		C		¹⁵T	E	¹⁶N	S	I	O	N		A
N		T			D		E		E		O			N			S
G		R			D		R		E		V			E			P
	¹⁷S	A	¹⁸S	S	Y		E		E		E			D			I
¹⁹S		R		I			N		D		L			²⁰M			N
A		Y		M			T			²¹S	T	A	L	K	I	N	G
R				U			²²A			Y				S			
²³C	²⁴O	M	P	L	I	C	A	T	E	D				C			
A	A			A			H			²⁵P	A	G	A	N			
S	N			T			E							S			
T	I			E			I			²⁶P	R	I	M	I	T	I	V	E
I	A			D			S										
C	C						²⁷T	O	L	E	R	A	T	E			

Across
1. Intense
3. Empty
11. Insight
12. A period of time
14. Inherited; inborn
15. Anxiety; unease
17. Lively
21. Walking in an angry manner
23. Difficult; involved
25. Person who worships many gods
26. Uncivilized; simple
27. Permit; endure

Down
2. Hit with a sharp blow
4. Supporters; partners
5. Deserted; left
6. Small amount of color
7. Napping
8. Example for future actions
9. Bothered; annoyed
10. Opposite
13. Harsh, grating sound
16. New and unusual thing
18. Imitation
19. Mocking
20. Put in an unsuitable role
22. One who does not believe in God
24. Madman; lunatic

VOCABULARY MATCHING *Rumble Fish*

Directions: Place the letter of the matching definition on the blank line.

____ 1. acute
____ 2. allies
____ 3. alternative
____ 4. atheist
____ 5. cautious
____ 6. complicated
____ 7. era
____ 8. eventually
____ 9. innate
____ 10. miscast
____ 11. novelty
____ 12. obnoxious
____ 13. precedent
____ 14. primitive
____ 15. scowling
____ 16. scrounging
____ 17. superelite
____ 18. tension
____ 19. throbbing
____ 20. tinge

A. put in an unsuitable role
B. a small amount of color
C. intense
D. inherited; inborn
E. searching for what can be found
F. careful
G. aching
H. difficult; involved
I. supporters; partners
J. example for future actions
K. high fashion
L. one who does not believe in God
M. anxiety; unease
N. offensive; annoying
O. a period of time
P. uncivilized; simple
Q. choice
R. a new and unusual thing
S. looking annoyed by lowering the eyebrows
T. finally

ANSWER KEY VOCABULARY MATCHING *Rumble Fish*

C	1.	acute	A.	put in an unsuitable role
I	2.	allies	B.	a small amount of color
Q	3.	alternative	C.	intense
L	4.	atheist	D.	inherited; inborn
F	5.	cautious	E.	searching for what can be found
H	6.	complicated	F.	careful
O	7.	era	G.	aching
T	8.	eventually	H.	difficult; involved
D	9.	innate	I.	supporters; partners
A	10.	miscast	J.	example for future actions
R	11.	novelty	K.	high fashion
N	12.	obnoxious	L.	one who does not believe in God
J	13.	precedent	M.	anxiety; unease
P	14.	primitive	N.	offensive; annoying
S	15.	scowling	O.	a period of time
E	16.	scrounging	P.	uncivilized; simple
K	17.	superelite	Q.	choice
M	18.	tension	R.	a new and unusual thing
G	19.	throbbing	S.	looking annoyed by lowering the eyebrows
B	20.	tinge	T.	finally

VOCABULARY MULTIPLE CHOICE *Rumble Fish*

1. **alone**
    a. abandoned
    b. vacant
    c. solitary
    d. cautious

2. **bothered; annoyed**
    a. throbbing
    b. pestered
    c. contrary
    d. maniac

3. **mocking**
    a. obnoxious
    b. acute
    c. rasping
    d. sarcastic

4. **napping**
    a. dozing
    b. scowling
    c. stalking
    d. scrounging

5. **lively**
    a. superelite
    b. acute
    c. sassy
    d. maniac

6. **walking in an angry manner**
    a. obnoxious
    b. stalking
    c. throbbing
    d. scrounging

7. **in a confused manner**
    a. distorted
    b. pestered
    c. sarcastic
    d. dazedly

8. **deformed; twisted out of shape**
    a. distorted
    b. innate
    c. novelty
    d. throbbing

9. **empty**
    a. vacant
    b. primitive
    c. rasping
    d. acute

10. **a gang fight**
    a. era
    b. tension
    c. pagan
    d. rumble

11. **madman; lunatic**
    a. atheist
    b. maniac
    c. pagan
    d. primitive

12. **imitation**
    a. primitive
    b. pagan
    c. contrary
    d. simulated

13. **permit; endure**
    a. tolerate
    b. contrary
    c. tinge
    d. simulated

14. **deserted; left**
    a. clipped
    b. pestered
    c. abandoned
    d. miscast

15. **hit with a sharp blow**
    a. tinge
    b. clipped
    c. complicated
    d. dozing

16. **insight**
    a. tinge
    b. era
    c. cautious
    d. perception

ANSWER KEY VOCABULARY MULTIPLE CHOICE *Rumble Fish*

1. alone
   a. abandoned
   b. vacant
   c. **solitary**
   d. cautious

2. bothered; annoyed
   a. throbbing
   b. **pestered**
   c. contrary
   d. maniac

3. mocking
   a. obnoxious
   b. acute
   c. rasping
   d. **sarcastic**

4. napping
   a. **dozing**
   b. scowling
   c. stalking
   d. scrounging

5. lively
   a. superelite
   b. acute
   c. **sassy**
   d. maniac

6. walking in an angry manner
   a. obnoxious
   b. **stalking**
   c. throbbing
   d. scrounging

7. confused
   a. distorted
   b. pestered
   c. sarcastic
   d. **dazedly**

8. deformed; twisted out of shape
   a. **distorted**
   b. innate
   c. novelty
   d. throbbing

9. empty
   a. **vacant**
   b. primitive
   c. rasping
   d. acute

10. a gang fight
    a. era
    b. tension
    c. pagan
    d. **rumble**

11. madman; lunatic
    a. atheist
    b. **maniac**
    c. pagan
    d. primitive

12. imitation
    a. primitive
    b. pagan
    c. contrary
    d. **simulated**

13. permit; endure
    a. **tolerate**
    b. contrary
    c. tinge
    d. simulated

14. deserted; left
    a. clipped
    b. pestered
    c. **abandoned**
    d. miscast

15. hit with a sharp blow
    a. tinge
    b. **clipped**
    c. complicated
    d. dozing

16. insight
    a. tinge
    b. era
    c. cautious
    d. **perception**

VOCABULARY WORD SCRAMBLE *Rumble Fish*

SCRAMBLE	**WORD**	**CLUE**
BOANEDDAN	ABANDONED	deserted; left
TAUEC	ACUTE	intense
SELLAI	ALLIES	supporters; partners
TLEVRAATIEN	ALTERNATIVE	choice
TISTAEH	ATHEIST	one who does not believe in God
ATICUSOU	CAUTIOUS	careful
LIPEDPC	CLIPPED	hit with a sharp blow
TCPLCOAMIED	COMPLICATED	difficult; involved
ONATRCRY	CONTRARY	opposite
LADEDYZ	DAZEDLY	confused
ITOERSTDD	DISTORTED	deformed; twisted out of shape
ZOIDNG	DOZING	napping
EAR	ERA	a period of time
LETEUNLYAV	EVENTUALLY	finally
TINAEN	INNATE	inherited; inborn
AIACMN	MANIAC	madman; lunatic
AMICSST	MISCAST	put in an unsuitable role
ELVTNYO	NOVELTY	new and unusual thing
BOIOUSOXN	OBNOXIOUS	searching offensive; annoying
AANPG	PAGAN	a person who worships many gods
CEEPTIPNRO	PERCEPTION	insight
PSEEEDTR	PESTERED	bothered; annoyed
TPNEREDCE	PRECEDENT	example for future actions
MIPTIVREI	PRIMITIVE	uncivilized; simple
GASPIRN	RASPING	a harsh, grating sound
BREUML	RUMBLE	gang fight
CARSTICAS	SARCASTIC	mocking
SSYSA	SASSY	lively
WINGSCOL	SCOWLING	looking angry by lowering the eyebrows
CONGRIUNSG	SCROUNGING	searching
IMDULATSE	SIMULATED	imitation
LOITRYSA	SOLITARY	alone
TAINSLGK	STALKING	walking in an angry manner
UEESLITERP	SUPERELITE	high-fashion
SENTINO	TENSION	anxiety; unease
HRBINGOTB	THROBBING	aching
INETG	TINGE	small amount of color
EOLRTETA	TOLERATE	permit; endure

www.ingramcontent.com/pod-product-compliance
Lightning Source LLC
Chambersburg PA
CBHW051411070526
44584CB00023B/3388